PRAISE FOR *LESS IS MORE*

"A fresh take on the business of producing real results." —*Fast Company*

"Refreshing, useful, and readable, [*Less Is More*] will help any entrepreneur get more done." —*Entrepreneur magazine*

"A great book that reads as easily as the best fiction . . . on a par with *Good to Great*." —Jack Covert, founder and president, 800-CEO-READ

"Great book . . . I read every word . . . Forget dull and boring, Jenning's new book is anything but. . . . Filled with useful advice."

—Al Ries, author of *The Fall of Advertising and the Rise of PR*

"Could easily be titled *The Seven Habits of Effective Organizations*. Terrific, fresh examples, accessible writing, and the crystal clear ring of truth. I will give this book to every new CEO and GM I know and hope they take heed." —Sam Hill, author of *Radical Marketing*

"In a world now troubled with recession, scandal, and panic, Jennings provides a welcome relief with his clarity and focus on business fundamentals." —Stan Davis , coauthor of *Blur* and *It's Alive: The Comimg Convergence of Information, Biology, and Business*

ABOUT THE AUTHOR

Worldwide bestselling author Jason Jennings is an advisor, consultant, and one of the world's most popular and in-demand business speakers. His books have been translated into twenty-three languages. When not traveling the globe on business assignments or adventure travel, he and his family live in Tiburon, California.

LESS IS MORE

How Great Companies Improve
Productivity Without Layoffs

JASON JENNINGS

PORTFOLIO

This book is dedicated to the businessmen and -women whose remarkable stories and achievements are revealed in its pages and the people who allowed me the privilege of leading them on a fascinating and humbling yearlong journey of discovery.

PORTFOLIO
Published by the Penguin Group
Penguin Group (USA) Inc., 375 Hudson Street, New York, New York 10014, U.S.A.
Penguin Books Ltd, 80 Strand, London WC2R 0RL, England
Penguin Books Australia Ltd, 250 Camberwell Road, Camberwell, Victoria 3124, Australia
Penguin Books Canada Ltd, 10 Alcorn Avenue, Toronto, Ontario, Canada M4V 3B2
Penguin Books India (P) Ltd, 11 Community Centre, Panchsheel Park, New Delhi–110 017, India
Penguin Books (N.Z.) Ltd, Cnr Rosedale and Airborne Roads, Albany, Auckland, New Zealand
Penguin Books (South Africa) (Pty) Ltd, 24 Sturdee Avenue,
    Rosebank, Johannesburg 2196, South Africa

Penguin Books Ltd, Registered Offices:
80 Strand, London WC2R 0RL, England

First published in the United States of America by Portfolio,
    a member of Penguin Putnam Inc. 2002
This paperback edition published 2004

10 9 8 7 6 5 4 3 2 1

PUBLISHER'S NOTE
This publication is designed to provide accurate and authoritative information in regard to the subject matter covered. It is sold with the understanding that the publisher is not engaged in rendering legal, accounting or other professional services. If you require legal advice or other expert assistance, you should seek the services of a competent professional.

THE LIBRARY OF CONGRESS HAS CATALOGUED THE HARDCOVER EDITION AS FOLLOWS:
Jennings, Jason.
    Less is more : how great companies use productivity as a competitive tool in business /
Jason Jennings.
        p.   cm.
    ISBN 1-59184-001-5 (hc.)
    ISBN 1-59184-030-9 (pbk.)
    1. Industrial productivity—Measurement. 2. Organizational effectiveness—
Measurement. 3. Performance—Measurement. I. Title.
HD56.25 .J456 2002
658.5'15—dc21   2002031177

Printed in the United States of America
Set in Berkeley with ITC Symbol display
Designed by Carla Bolte

CONTENTS

FOREWORD

Given the continuing unparalleled performance of the companies we wrote about in the original edition of *Less Is More* I believe, more than ever, that this book should be read and studied by everyone who has anything to do with business. The companies and the remarkable people who lead them have proven themselves—again!—to be the best and most productive business organizations on the planet.

It's Been Rough . . . For Everyone

During the bust that followed the boom of the late nineties, most businesses dug in their heels and struggled to stay alive. Between 2001 and 2003, U.S. corporate profits tumbled more than 20 percent and most businesses had to work overtime to even come close to achieving their performance of the previous year(s). We saw wave upon wave of layoffs, downsizings, reorganizations, and slashed spending. We heard the death knells for new initiatives, and threatened beheadings for anyone with the temerity to suggest an investment in IT. Trillions of dollars of shareholder value went up in smoke and for hundreds of thousands of businesses, the struggle proved futile and fatal.

By contrast, every company we researched and wrote about in the original edition has not only survived but has prospered. Despite facing the same economy as everyone else, each of these companies grew revenues, increased profits, collectively added tens of thousands of jobs, introduced new products and services, bought other companies, and continued the march onward and upward. It's because they do things right.

Still the Most Productive Companies in the World

World Savings

When I first wrote about Herb and Mary Sandler, the co-chairs and CEOs of World Savings for more than forty years, I described their financial institution as a place where egos are checked at the door. Most significantly, World Savings attracts twice the number of deposits to their branches as their nearest competitor, while simultaneously operating their branch network for half the expense. World Savings was the only company in the world we were able to identify that has increased their earnings per share at an annualized rate of 20 percent per year for thirty-five years.

Even after the U.S. economy officially fell into recession after September 11, World Savings has continued their incredibly strong performance and expects to grow their operating income by a full 30 percent between December 2001 and December 2003.

Nucor Steel

It would be difficult to find a business sector more battered by cyclical economies than the steel industry. Since 1997 more than forty U.S. steel companies have declared bankruptcy. Hardly a week goes by that steel company CEOs aren't in Washington, D.C., with begging bowls in hand, asking the government to maintain tariffs on imported steel or begging for the government to take over their depleted pension funds. Traditional steel companies argue they can't compete because of their burdensome legacy costs: pensions, union contracts, old mills and furnaces. Not so for Nucor Steel.

Since we first researched and wrote about Nucor Steel they've confronted the same big problems experienced by the rest of the industry, but have chosen to address them in a different way. They recently announced their 123rd consecutive quarterly dividend (thirty-one straight years of profitability); in April 2002 they entered a joint venture with Mitsubishi Corporation and a Chinese steel maker to construct a plant in Australia and they purchased Birmingham Steel and its four operating mills with an annual capacity of 2,000,000 tons.

During the recession and bear market of 2001 to 2003, nonresidential construction in the U.S. hit the skids and adversely affected Nucor's steel girder business. But, defying all odds, in the past twelve months the company has still increased revenue by double digits (10 percent) and grew profits by 43 percent over the previous year.

Ryanair

Since September 11, various members of the financial and business press have estimated that the world's airlines have collectively lost more than $30 billion. That's more money than the industry has earned in total since aviation began. The havoc caused by terrorism, disease, and recession guarantees that airlines will struggle, reorganize, revamp, and dodge for cover in bankruptcy court for years to come.

When we first identified Ryanair as one of the most productive companies in the world, this Irish discount airline was already beating Southwest Airlines, the premiere discount carrier in the U.S., by nearly 4 to 1 in every operating metric. Since that time, with nearly all other airlines in bankruptcy or teetering on the edge, the continuing triumphs achieved by Ryanair would fill a record book.

Ryanair has launched service to twenty new destinations in the past twelve months. In the same time, Ryanair has continued to be Europe's number one on-time airline, number one for fewest lost bags, and number one in punctuality when compared to all U.S. airlines. The number of people flying Ryanair grew by nearly 40 percent, to 15 million in fiscal 2002–2003, while revenues grew a stunning 35 percent and they achieved an after tax profit margin of 28 percent. Aviation history was made when the company announced the world's largest order (150 new airplanes) for Boeing 737s.

Ryanair is arguably the world's best example of how to use a single big objective to motivate people and build a culture. This company is determined to become Europe's largest schedule international carrier with 40 million passengers annually by 2010. I'm taking all bets they'll accomplish it.

The Warehouse Group

Wal-Mart is constantly hailed as the world's most efficient and profitable retailer, so you can imagine the skepticism shared by the research team and me when we uncovered a retail organization based in New Zealand and Australia that beats Wal-Mart in almost every operational metric.

Two years have past since our initial research on The Warehouse Group and their 230 retail locations across Australasia. Despite a recent unexplained hiccup in the office of the CEO, which saw Stephen Tindall, the company's founder, stepping back into his previous role, The Warehouse Group continues to handily beat Wal-Mart in the key Return on Equity category by 20 percent, turning in an extraordinarily high ROE of 27 percent. In the past twelve months they've increased sales 12 percent over year earlier figures, grew earnings per share a whopping 33 percent, and increased their dividend by 8 percent.

Yellow Corp.

In 2003, Yellow Corp. was chosen as America's number one most admired company in its sector by *Fortune* magazine. It's an amazing accomplishment for a company to go from teetering on the edge of a cliff to becoming one of the world's most productive companies, and then its most admired, in only seven years.

Despite a dismal economy that witnessed the collapse of other transportation companies, Yellow Corp. again managed to significantly grow revenues and double their earnings per share in 2002 and in 2003 announced the acquisition of a rival firm, Roadway, for nearly one billion dollars.

IKEA

The numbers say it all for this well-oiled, privately held retail machine. During the past twelve months the group has opened six new stores, added more than 10,000 workers, and grew sales by more than 22 percent to a $12 billion annual clip. They also plan to open five new stores annually in the U.S for the next ten years, and have expanded into Shanghai, China.

While every company written about surpasses the expectations of their customers, IKEA has turned the art of customer satisfaction into a science. Every employee lives the life of their target customers—the masses—instead of sitting in an ivory tower and pretending to know what their customers want.

SRC Holdings

No parent or grandparent would ever admit to having a favorite but, despite my respect and deep admiration for every company and leader written about in the following pages, only SRC's CEO Jack Stack can bring me to tears by the magnitude of the pure authenticity he radiates.

SRC takes some of the dirtiest and un-sexiest businesses in the world and turns them into ultramodern, highly disciplined business units. Stack's goal is a simple one: make every worker economically, financially, and business literate and savvy so they truly understand how the business works.

Last year, annual revenues at SRC were up another double digit—16 percent—and operating profit increased 36 percent in the tradition of a company where you'd expect nothing less.

Recently, while flying on a cramped commuter airline between Springfield and St. Louis, Missouri, I was impressed by a young man whose keyboarding on his laptop wasn't even interrupted by the violent thunderstorms we were passing through. As we approached our landing, I asked him what company he worked for. "I work for SRC Holdings," he replied, adding, "the greatest company in the world."

Lantech

We originally touted privately held Lantech as the model of efficiency and productivity; it was a company where they'd managed to increase productivity 1 percent a month for seven years and triple sales without increasing staff.

Of all the companies we studied, Lantech was perhaps the most vulnerable to a bad economy. As you'll learn, they build devices that make big boxes out of lots of little boxes, so that manufacturers can more easily ship their goods and products to end destinations. It simply stands to reason that when manufacturers are building and shipping less they'd have fewer needs for the innovative equipment designed and built by Lantech. If you think that sounds like a reason for a dip in productivity at Lantech, you'd be wrong.

The most recent twelve-month numbers reveal how chairman Pat Lancaster and his son Jim, the company CEO, outwitted a dismal economy. As further testament to the firm's relentless commitment to constantly increasing productivity, during the past year the firm has increased revenues 4 percent, shipments 19 percent, profits 15 percent, and sales per employee a remarkable 20 percent, all while improving their safety numbers a full 50 percent. It's clear that Lantech responded to decreased demand and greater competition by striving for nothing short of constant improvement. This allowed them to reduce costs, pass along a substantial portion of the savings realized to their buyers, and achieve even higher levels of productivity per employee while being simultaneously committed to safety. That's the very definition of productivity: increasing the output while maintaining or decreasing the input without putting anyone in physical danger.

You'll gain an entirely new perspective on courageous leadership when you read about Pat Lancaster's productivity epiphany and how any one company can duplicate the success they've achieved at Lantech.

What About Wall Street?

The question I'm most frequently asked is, "Would you recommend buying the stocks of the companies you wrote about in *Less Is More*?"

Some people ask the question out of genuine curiosity, others because they're seeking a hot investment tip, and I suspect a few are asking it as a "gotcha" question, hopeful that some of the companies have faltered. Before responding to their question, I always provide the following admonition.

Anyone who buys a stock based on a hot tip or the advice of a stranger is a fool. The only companies worthy of investment are those with authentic leadership, a demonstrated ability to sustain momentum in good times and bad, the restraint to constantly control costs, and an insatiable *ménage a trois* between leaders, employees, and customers. Any prospective investment that fulfills those criteria is bound to be a good one.

But, that said, I delight to answer with a resounding yes; yes, all the publicly traded stocks we wrote about two years ago have outperformed their peers and collectively outperformed the market handsomely. On September 1, 2001, if an investor with $100,000 had purchased $20,000 in each of the five publicly traded companies we wrote about—Nucor, World Savings, Yellow Corp., The Warehouse Group, and Ryanair—and then held the stocks and reinvested any dividends, on June 30, 2003 the investor's portfolio would have been worth $129,000. By comparison, the same $100,000 invested in the S&P500, which accounts for 80 percent of all stock market activity would have been worth $87,000 meaning an investment in the companies profiled in the following pages performed 48 percent better than the overall market. So, sometimes, even the markets prove they make sense.

The Search Continues

As you read these words, a newly-formed research team headed by Brian Solon, a recent UC Berkeley MBA, and I are deep in the midst of evaluating more than 100,000 publicly traded and privately owned companies, searching for ten who do "something" better than anyone else—if we told you what that "something" was we'd have to kill you—for our next book from Portfolio, scheduled for release in early 2005. We'll be traipsing the world trying to learn how these companies manage to do what they do so well, and then report the results to you. The research team and I invite you to visit www.jennings-solutions.com for ongoing progress reports.

I'm gratified and humbled that our hardcover version of *Less Is More* became a national bestseller, but I won't feel completely fulfilled until every businessperson on the planet has a dog-eared paperback in their possession, asking all the questions posed in this remarkable little book. Please spread the word . . . less is indeed more!

—Jason Jennings
July 2003
Tiburon, California

INTRODUCTION

Productivity—What's It All About?

It's about maintaining output while decreasing input. Or, better still, increasing output while decreasing input. Bottom line: getting more done with the same or less!

Efficiency and productivity have always fascinated me—as they must anyone in business. But each time I tried tackling a book on the subject, I was either bored to death by all the charts, tables, half-page-long, small-type footnotes—big yawn—or cowed by the esoteric, highbrow academic nature of the subject and all the explanations of macroeconomics, percentage shares of this and that, proposed pro forma operational cost measures—nap time—and references to cross-company processing. All the math and jargon made my hair hurt.

Why wasn't there a book about how the most efficient and productive companies got that way, with lessons that anyone or any company could follow?

Once I made the decision to fill that gap, the mission became obvious: identify some of the most productive companies in the world, dig deep inside, learn what they do differently from and better than their less productive rivals and then describe the lessons learned, in a way that other businesspeople could easily understand and implement.

The Search Begins

I began by assembling a team of enthusiastic researchers (including recent graduates of Princeton, Stanford and Berkeley) and setting them and me the task of examining thousands of companies around the world with no preconceived criteria in mind. The team members would simply keep open eyes and minds as we searched tens of thousands of databases, public records, financial reports, archived stories and previously published articles. We would identify those companies where even a hint of efficiency, thrift or productivity was noted.

Over a matter of months we developed a prospective list of eighty companies with performances that were far better than those of others. We made our selections after examining, considering, discussing and discarding thousands as being "same old, same old."

Then the researchers spent weeks studying a group of the companies assigned to them individually, eventually presenting their best arguments to the entire team for each business they thought should be considered for further research and inclusion in the book. The team members knew that questioning would be incisive and their answers had to be precise. We were determined to be tough on each other. The intensity built and the researchers treated the project as seriously as an adventure in survival—intellectual survival, but survival nonetheless.

Throughout this process, the criteria for being included slowly developed and were refined as the vetting process continued. Did a company's *sales per employee* exceed the average for the industry category? If not, the group argued, it would be hard to present a case for productivity. Did the firm's *return on invested capital* exceed or lead the field for its respective business category or group? What about profits? Unless a firm's *profit per employee* was superior to its competitors', it'd be tough building a case for world-class productivity. Had they done something—anything—that made them more productive than their peers? If they were not deemed outstanding, they were dumped.

Soon another criterion—an offbeat one—began to surface.

"Ugh, what a boring company," said one of the researchers. "Who in the heck would want to read about *that* outfit?"

I began to wonder if "sex appeal" should be a selection criterion. If a company didn't have some kind of sparkle, the reader would be much less likely to respond to the story, no matter how valid the ideas. The research, interviewing and writing might grow into a tedious chore instead of an adventure, and I'd be hard put to convince the reader to care. So if this book were to become a page-turner, style and attractiveness of the companies would have to count in the selection process.

And since we wouldn't be naming and defending the selected companies as the *only* productive companies in the world, we would be free to choose the ones that made the most exciting reading. Our list would include about ten of the most productive businesses on the planet—ones we fervently believed possessed lessons that could be used by other people in business.

So after all the musing and sifting, what were the criteria we finally settled on as the standards for judging productivity? What are the measures that show whether a company and its employees are outperforming the rest of the pack in the areas that truly matter?

What Makes a Productive Company—the Criteria

Here's our list of criteria for selecting the companies included in the book:

■ **Revenue Per Employee**

This measure—arrived at by dividing total sales by the number of employees—speaks volumes about a company's ability to efficiently market and sell its goods. (One company on our initial list, the hot Spanish fashion retailer Zara, gets a lot of great press, but generates only $100,000 in annual sales per employee, while the average fashion retailer generates $302,000. It simply didn't measure up.)

We also became aware of a ploy some companies use to inflate their sales per employee numbers. They fire employees and rehire them or others as a contracted workforce. It looks good on paper but it didn't get past us. We counted the workforce numbers of all the companies we eventually profiled to make certain they were accurate and we tallied part-time employees and proportionately counted them as full-time equivalents.

▪ Return on Equity and Return on Assets

The percentage return on a company's net worth for a given period tells shareholders how effectively capital is being employed. For example, if a company's net worth (assets less liabilities) is $5 million and they earn $1 million in a year, their annual return on equity is 20 percent.

During our research, we analyzed many companies that earned substantial profits and provided competitive returns on their stockholders' equity. But some of the returns on equity we unearthed were mammoth by comparison to industry or business averages, indicating that these companies are far superior to their rivals in either their efficiencies or their productivity.

Similarly we reviewed a company's return on assets and only the top performers made our final list.

▪ Operating Income Per Employee

When comparing companies, net profit numbers can be misleading: they're affected by differing national tax rates and often include a myriad of one-time charges or credits that may not be a reflection of actual income from operations. So we decided instead to use income from operations divided by the number of full-time, or full-time equivalent, employees, which seems a much better indication of a company's productivity.

This criterion gives an edge to companies that pay their workers poorly, are notoriously cheap or beat up their suppliers on a regular basis. While this book is about doing more with less and not about being nice or winning popularity contests, we also believe the marketplace is ultimately fair, rewards value and punishes bad operators. We required our chosen companies to have proven themselves by having been in business for ten years or more, which should mean we got rid of the chiselers.

And then we identified two other criteria that lean to the emotional rather than the intellectual:

■ Has the company been overexposed?

Three companies—Nokia, Southwest Airlines and Harley-Davidson—made our final cut but were not the subject of extensive in-depth research by our team. This way we walk on largely untrampled ground and avoid focusing on businesses that have been widely written about.

■ Might this company pull an Enron?

In light of the spectacular collapse of Enron, which went from being America's high-flying seventh-largest company into the Dumpster in a matter of months, we were eager to avoid Tom Peters's embarrassment when a number of excellent companies sagged badly soon after publication of *In Search of Excellence*.

So, based on all the other criteria, a tentative final list of companies was compiled and given to a team of CPAs with the admonition to look at the companies' public data, take it apart, put it back together again and provide as much assurance as possible that each of the companies was strong and likely to endure.

The Survivors Are . . .

We ended up with a surprising mix of companies.

- A European airline that outperforms Southwest Airlines by every standard of measurement.
- A manufacturing company that managed to increase productivity 1 percent a month for seven years, tripled sales without increasing staff and slashed the production cycle for a piece of equipment from five weeks to eleven hours.
- A chain of discount stores in New Zealand and Australia that puts twice as much profit per sales dollar to the bottom line as Wal-Mart and nearly doubles Wal-Mart's return on equity.
- A steelmaker that has slashed the length of time it takes to produce a ton of steel by more than 90 percent, has never had a layoff, pays its workers 30 to 40 percent more than the industry average and has still turned in 132 consecutive quarters of profitability in an industry where twenty of its competitors have gone bankrupt within the past three years.
- A company in America's Midwest founded with a debt-to-equity ratio of 89 to 1, whose chances for survival were slim to none. Today the company grows 15 percent every year, in good times and bad, and credits its success to the financial statement that's posted on huge white boards in the cafeterias. Everyone in the company—even the factory workers—can read a P&L and a balance sheet, and all attend weekly meetings to review every line of the statements including the balance in the bank.
- A furniture retailer based in Sweden and Denmark that achieves annual profits per employee of an astounding one hundred thou-

sand dollars—twenty-five times the industry average—and whose frugal owner shops at the produce market late in the day when the prices are cheaper even though he's worth $30 billion. He says, "It's about staying close to the common man."

- A financial institution that generates a staggering $762,000 per employee per year, where not a penny is wasted on the trappings of power and general and administrative expenses are half those of other banks. Led by a feisty couple in their early seventies, this bank won't even talk to salespeople no matter what they're selling, because it takes up valuable time. "Submit everything in writing, please."

- A trucking company that sat perched on the edge of the grave only five years ago and has reinvented itself as an efficient leader in transportation solutions. It's a fascinating story of how the top executives had to leave before great things could happen.

The Field Research

Some people who head highly productive companies are afraid their competitive advantage might disappear if their rivals learn about and copy what they do. Gaining access to a few of them was one of the toughest tasks I've faced.

Others, however, greeted with open arms the chance to be part of the book and cooperated in every way possible.

I spent a lot of time wondering why some were so secretive and others so welcoming. Then late one night, on a bumpy airplane ride in a small plane across America's Midwest, the simple answer occurred to me: some companies had dirty little secrets they didn't want seen in the light of day.

The CEOs who had genuinely mastered productivity were, without exception, cooperative and open. CEOs with something to hide were not. We aggressively pursued every company, even those where gaining admittance was difficult, but in each instance where we had to fight very hard to get in the door, our efforts proved less than fruitful. In the case of a highly lauded chain of women's fashion retailers we discovered they produced their goods in poor Central American nations for twenty-five cents an hour, slapped MADE IN MEXICO labels on them and smuggled them into the United States under the banner of NAFTA. We knew what we'd find if we picked away at that scab any further. In the case of a computer manufacturer that claims $1 million per year per employee in revenue we eventually discovered they didn't count more than 70 percent of their workers as employees but instead as contract labor, which grossly distorted their numbers. And eventually we abandoned our research of a grocery chain when it became clear the company had an institutionalized policy of discrimination against women in the management ranks. This was to be a study about productivity, not dinosaurs and fossils.

Rather than drop from our list the one company where our access to the CEO was limited to an exchange of faxes, we relied on solid research, the public record and interviews with employees, customers, vendors, suppliers and former executives.

Our Ambition and Wish

I passionately believe that the lessons the research team and I learned from these companies will prove that *Less Is More* and show you how to become more efficient and productive in your business and your life.

Enjoy the read. I strongly encourage you to use the lessons that you will learn and put them into practice as fast as you can!

—Jason Jennings, 2002

FOCUS

1

A Simple BIG Objective

In the absence of a simple BIG objective to act as a unifying force, no leader or manager can hope to make a company more productive.

—Bill Zollars, CEO, Yellow Corp.

Before committing even one word to paper, as I led my research team to begin the initial work of identifying a group of the world's most productive companies and figuring out how they do what they do, I'd have never guessed—not in a million years—what the theme would turn out to be for this opening chapter.

After all, the book was intended as a collection of the tactics employed by these firms to be more efficient than other businesses, proving the proposition that *Less Is More*. I'd imagined getting right into things with machine gun staccato . . . *bang, they do this, bang, bang, they do that, bang, bang, bang!*

Then a big discovery went *boom* and got in the way of my plans. Here it is: In productive companies, the culture *is* the strategy.

As I crisscrossed the United States and traveled the world, hanging out with the customers, workers, managers and leaders of companies where less is more, a single indisputable fact kept confronting me:

Unlike other companies, productive companies know the difference between tactics and strategy.

That difference is the foundation that allows them to stay focused and build remarkable companies. They have institutionalized their strategy.

There's a lot of *bang, bang, bang* stuff in the chapters to follow but, as a result of our exhaustive research, I'm convinced that a company will never become truly productive unless the management can learn to nail down the differences between strategy and tactics and allow the strategy to become the culture.

Strategy du Jour

If you keep your ears open on airplanes, at business meetings and in boardrooms, you'll hear the word "strategy" tossed around so frequently as to render it meaningless. It seems everyone has a strategy for *this,* a strategy for *that,* a strategy for everything from dealing with the kids to buying a new laptop to handling the boss . . . and yep, one for being more productive. And how many people do you know who have climbed the corporate ladder because management (or human resources) identified them as "strategic thinkers"?

What's even more alarming is the frequency with which companies discard one "strategy" for another in the name of being flexible. Grasping at tactic after tactic, trying this and trying that and incorrectly labeling everything they attempt as a "strategy," most companies cloud the climate, confuse the troops and do the opposite of what it takes to be productive. Productive companies keep everything clear and simple—everything *including* strategy.

As I came to the end of my in-depth interviews with the CEOs of the companies covered in this book, I was struck by the fact that each shared this in common; the ownership of and fierce loyalty to a very simple big objective. The big objective *was* the strategy and it became the culture; everything else was tactics on how to achieve it.

All of these leaders vigorously prevent anyone from mucking up their drive for productivity with some strategy du jour or the latest alphabet-soup management theory.

Imagine for a moment the power of everyone in your organization—whether a ten-employee restaurant or a thirty-thousand-worker transportation company—knowing and striving to achieve a simple big objective.

While having everyone in a company share this simple BIG objective might seem to be simply common sense, as the age-old maxim goes, the most common thing about common sense . . . is how uncommon it is.

So what are these strategies—these BIG objectives—that are held so firmly by the leaders of some of the most productive businesses in the world?

NOPE! It's Not That Vision Thing Again

People who have survived the mission and vision thing give a knowing grin and agree that most of those grandiose statements are fit only to be framed on the wall of the reception area, put on the cover of the annual report and talked about with the head honcho to show you're on the team. They definitely are not ideas anybody would actually try to carry out to get the job done better. Unfortunately, lofty mission and vision statements, like all the other empty promises too many companies make, have a rich history of not being worth squat.

The real grunt work involved in building a productive company doesn't happen in the boardroom or executive offices; it's done on the shop floor, in the offices, on the factory line, on the retail sales floor and in the field. The very people who have the ability to make a business more productive have "been there, seen that, done that" with the vision thing.

The Power of a Simple BIG Objective

One company that's a poster child for productivity, Lantech, based in Louisville, Kentucky, discovered the need for a simple BIG objective the hard way.

The traditional means for a company to ready their product for shipment involve putting the individual units in boxes, putting lots of little boxes together to make a big box, then wrapping these big boxes in plastic sheeting and sending them through a heated tunnel to form a weatherproof shrink-wrap. When the big boxes come out of the tunnel, they're stacked on a pallet for forklifting onto a truck or railcar.

During the U.S. energy crisis of the 1970s, Lantech founder and chairman Pat Lancaster came up with the idea of wrapping pallets of boxes tightly with strong plastic from a continuous roll. (Picture wrapping a rubber band around your fingers a number of times.) The process meant no more need for shrink-wrap heating, which translated into significant energy savings. Patenting this process and equipment designs, the company spent the 1980s making money hand over fist. Lantech was (excuse the pun) on a roll. Today it's the world leader in stretch wrappers, palletizers and conveyor systems.

That's the bright side of the story but there was a dark side, as well. By Lancaster's admission the company wasn't doing a very good job in a lot of areas. "Quality and customer service were poor, the factory was inefficient, but there was so much demand that we just kept doing things the same old way."

Until one day in 1990. "After arguments all the way to the Supreme Court," he says, "we lost our patent protection and overnight everything changed. We had to admit to ourselves that we'd been selling *wheelbarrows* and been pretty arrogant about it. All of a sudden everybody else could sell the *same* wheelbarrow. It would no longer be enough to say we didn't suck worse than our competition."

Pat Lancaster realized in the dark of night and in the bright light of day that the company's free ride had ended. Unless he could dramatically reduce inventories, improve product quality, deliver superior customer service and become more productive, the days of Lantech as a company were numbered.

During the next ten years, Lantech tripled sales without increasing staff, slashed the time it took to build a single machine from five weeks to eleven hours(!), and increased productivity 1 percent a month for the entire time period—all because of one man's focus.

Pat Lancaster's simple BIG objective was to become the most efficient and productive manufacturing plant on the planet and do things better than they'd ever been done.

What? A Company More Productive Than Wal-Mart? Where?

In 1982, New Zealander Stephen Tindall founded The Warehouse, a single-location discount store in Auckland. Fast-forward twenty years and you'll find this publicly traded chain of two hundred stores across New Zealand and Australia outperforming America's Wal-Mart in every metric of productivity. While Wal-Mart puts 3.3 pennies of each sales dollar to the bottom line, The Warehouse puts 6.6. And while Wal-Mart achieves a stunning 24 percent return on equity, The Warehouse smokes them with a killer 40 percent.

At first glance you might think the success of The Warehouse is about technology, but dig deeper and you'll learn it all began and continues to exist because of a powerful simple BIG objective.

In 1982 Tindall, working for another department store, was on a buying trip to the United States and was accompanying a vendor on a supply run to a suburban New Jersey shopping center. When he saw his first suburban discount store, a light went off and he rushed home to New Zealand to quit his job and open his own store.

He took his entire life savings of forty thousand dollars, rented a large old industrial-area warehouse—hence the name—and plopped down thirty thousand dollars of his start-up capital for two computerized checkout terminals. If you're wondering, as I did, where he came up with the money to stock merchandise, you'll understand why he needed the two terminals.

Tindall saw he wouldn't have money for inventory so he went to all the companies he knew that had goods sitting in their own warehouses and offered a proposition. "Put your goods in my warehouse and I'll sell them for you," he pitched prospective vendors, arguing that the stuff wasn't doing them any good sitting unsold where it was. Then, brandishing his computerized inventory and checkout system, he promised to pay them weekly for whatever he sold. The caveat was that if he didn't sell it he could return it, eventually earning him the nickname "Sell-or-Return Stephen."

"Since the day we opened the doors in our first store," Tindall says, "this company has been an enterprise where people come first." But when Tindall says the words, the needle on the B.S. meter doesn't budge. You instinctively know he's telling the truth and want to hear more.

"Look," he continues, sounding a bit like a modern-day Robin Hood, "New Zealand, where we began, is a small island nation and much of what we sell has to be imported. As a result of manufacturers, manufacturers' reps, importers and their agents all taking their markups, the New Zealand consumer was constantly getting screwed and people ended up paying far too much for the goods they purchased."

He quickly showed he'd found a better way. "As soon as I'd proven that my concept for The Warehouse would work, I immediately began applying for licenses to become a direct importer in as many categories as I was able. Do you know the thrill," he asks, "of being able to sell a set of luggage for one-quarter of the department store's price and still end up with a higher margin than theirs?" Tindall chuckles and says, "Now, that's real fun."

But Tindall becomes his most emphatic when he proclaims, "It's not as much about selling merchandise as it is about empowering people and *giving the common working person the same choices that the wealthy always had*. That's the reason this company exists!"

Today, with his billion-dollar personal fortune, Stephen Tindall can dress, drive and do as he pleases. And he does, with a seventeen-dollar sport watch because "I swim every day and it's a great watch in the water," driving a Volkswagen because "I really like the shape" and living in a modest house he and his wife bought years ago. "Why do we need more house?" he asks.

Originally, the research team had a hypothesis that people heading highly productive companies might be personally thrifty (or cheap) and that their abhorrence of waste was in some part responsible for the creation of efficient enterprises. That's not what we found.

Instead, we found people who conduct their personal lives in harmony with the stated BIG objective. When I pushed Stephen Tindall on the issue of whether personal thrift is a precursor of productivity, he said, "I don't think so." But he added, "It would be pretty silly of me to run a company for the benefit of the common man and ask everyone around me to do the same if I weren't one myself, don't you think?"

"Thanks for Calling Yellow, Have a Nice Day"

When Bill Zollars was recruited from Ryder Trucks in the late nineties to become CEO of Yellow Corp., a *Fortune* 500 company, he found a troubled business that had stumbled badly since deregulation of the trucking industry. What disturbed him most was discovering that the company was very inwardly focused and had no measurements of customer satisfaction. Seeing that the company was coming off three years of extremely poor performances made worse by a strike and losses, Zollars recognized he would need to operate in turnaround mode.

Like Lantech, Yellow Corp. had been buffeted by government regulation. Zollars recalls that in the regulated environment where Yellow had prospered, companies never had to worry about strategies or customers. "If you needed more money, you just sent out a letter that said, 'Hey, I need a price increase,' and you got it. The business had become completely commoditized and the company that got the business was the last one in with a load of doughnuts or free tickets to a ballgame."

The effects of deregulation were entirely predictable, Zollars says. Lots of new people came in with great ideas, they opened new companies and raised the bar, so that many of the existing businesses couldn't compete and eventually went bust. Industry analysts, he says, were forecasting Yellow Corp.'s eventual demise. "The question I got asked most frequently when I got here," Zollars told me with a grin, "was whether we'd be around in a couple of years."

So what had Zollars spotted as clues he could use to keep that from happening? From his early days at the company, he noticed, "When people would ask someone who worked for Yellow what the company did, they'd respond by saying it was in the long-haul LTL trucking business." (LTL, or less than truckload, describes a carrier that specializes in shipments under a certain weight, combining shipments from several customers to make up each full truckload.)

Even today, Zollars fumes as he remembers. "Where's the pride and potential in being in the long-haul LTL trucking business? Not only are you putting yourself in a box, you're putting yourself in a really *little* box."

His answer to the many dilemmas facing the company was a strategy, a simple BIG objective. "We are not in the long-haul LTL trucking business," he commanded. Contrasting Yellow with two major competitors, he told his people, "We're going to get out of the trucking business and into the service business. And from now on, instead of wasting our time comparing ourselves to Roadway and Consolidated Freight, we're going to compare ourselves to Starbucks."

Starbucks! That's picking a successful model to emulate.

You've probably heard the remark that if the railroad companies had understood they weren't in the rail business but in the business of transporting people and goods, the airlines today would have names like Union Pacific or Santa Fe. Zollars instinctively understood the distinction.

Today he argues that until you get the "people thing" right, no amount of technology can make you more productive. "Look," he says, "we spend as much as eighty million dollars annually on technology, but it won't do a damn bit of good and make us more productive if the people using it don't *get* it.

"During my first week on the job," he told me, "I went to one of our state-of-the-art customer service centers in Des Moines, Iowa, and spent a day listening in on phone calls from our customers." With a knowing wink, he added, "You know darn well they put me with our best customer service people, not a newbie or an old crank."

What he heard made his ears burn. "A customer called and said he had a shipment that had to get from Chicago to Atlanta in two days. And our customer service person tells him we can get it there in three days. The customer repeats, 'No, I really need it there in two days,' and our customer service rep says again, 'We can get it there in three days.' Finally the customer says, 'Okay, I'll call someone else,' and our agent says, 'Okay, thanks for calling Yellow and letting us serve you. Have a nice day.'"

Zollars's comment: "Imagine a 'Thanks for letting us serve you,' when the agent had just sent the customer to our competition!"

Here's the way he saw the picture: "The entire mind-set of this company was, 'Here's what we do . . . if you want it, fine . . . if you don't, that's fine, too.' No one ever asked a customer what he or she wanted or needed. How can you ever hope to become productive until you get people on your side?" he asks.

Zollars's simple BIG objective was to get Yellow out of the trucking business and into the *service* business.

The Great Game of Business

Jack Stack is the CEO of SRC Holdings. Twenty years ago, as a young production whiz for International Harvester, he was sent to Missouri to run Springfield Remanufacturing Corporation, a business unit that rebuilt dirty broken-down engines into like-brand-new and sold them for 60 percent of the cost of a new one.

While Stack was turning around the facility and making it profitable, parent company Harvester was harvesting themselves into a deep mess, eventually trying to recover from owing the banks billions by chucking assets and laying off tens of thousands of people—in time eliminating more than 100,000 workers out of 115,000.

During that huge, gory bloodletting, workers would come to Stack and say, "What should I do?" "Should I buy a new car?" "Should I get married?" "Will I have a job?"

Finally, Stack responded to the pain of his people. Deciding, "This is bullshit," he went to them and said, "Look, don't buy the new car and don't get married. One of three things is going to happen. Harvester can sell us, they can close us or we'll all die a slow death from them not being able to supply our capital needs."

But Stack also offered hope in one other possibility. "I went around and asked people if we should try to buy the company from Harvester. I kept waiting for someone to say no. Nobody did and so we made an offer."

At the time, Stack's total net worth was $28,000 and he needed to raise $9 million. Banding together with a dozen other managers in the company, he was able to scrape together $100,000 for the down payment on a $9 million purchase. Then Stack embarked on a grueling, two-year search for financing that changed his life.

"I was out there looking for this huge pile of money and the bankers had me jumping through hoops and learning a new vocabulary," he remembers. "All of a sudden, out of nowhere, came things like equity ratios, liquidity ratios, debt financing and bonds. I'd always thought you kept the accountants and finance people in the back room and they did whatever they wanted with the numbers. The more I got into it, the more I loved it and thought, 'Wow, all this stuff with the numbers is great, it's a really neat system.'"

This led him to the conclusion that "the only way to win is by performance."

During Stack's time in the field, two things happened. "First," he says, "I was like a kid in a candy store. I loved learning about business. It got so that I could write and rewrite business plans in the back of a taxicab between pitches to bankers."

But during his search for financing, Stack also got mad. "I was completely angry with the company I'd worked for, for fourteen years. During my entire time with them, they'd never taught me business and never asked me to make money or generate cash. I could manufacture whatever they wanted me to make. I could build engines. I could make fifty-ton trucks. But I didn't know a darn thing about making money."

On February 1, 1983, when Stack and his co-owners got their factory, they had $100,000 in equity and $8.9 million in debt. His first order of business was to gather all three hundred workers together in a lunchroom and tell them that although they had jobs for the moment, the company was essentially comatose.

He explained to them that at a debt to equity ratio of 89 to 1, the company was brain-dead, but that if they were able to turn that number upside down and have 89 times more equity than debt, that was where real wealth would be found.

"I was so excited by what I'd learned that I wanted to share it with everyone," Stack recalls. "I knew cash-flow statements, income statements, balance sheets, I'd learned the lingo of the venture capitalists, the commercial bankers and the angel capitalists."

What he'd learned, he would share. "That day I made a promise to teach business to every worker in the company."

The factory workers, the managers and even the other executives were all as much in the dark about business as Stack had been. "We'd all thought it was about building great products, that it was only about delivery, quality, service and housekeeping—but along the way we'd missed the boat. We'd been kept in a jungle of making stuff but had never been allowed to see the big picture."

Stack made good on his promise to teach everyone business, with steps that include calling the whole company together weekly for a detailed update on the firm's profit and loss statement and balance sheet. Today a visit to any SRC facility starts in the lunchroom where an entire wall details the company's financial statement including how much money they have in the bank. As you walk the factory floor engaging people in conversation, you find workers who are as comfortable talking price-equity as pistons, cash flows as cylinders.

SRC Holdings has become a widely diversified manufacturing holding company that grows 15 percent per year in good times and bad, whose twenty-two plants are involved in fifteen different manufacturing operations. With revenues greater than $200 million annually, the company handily beats their competitors on all the productivity metrics—revenue per employee, operating income per employee and return on invested capital.

Stack's simple BIG objective was to teach everyone the rules of business and then turn it into a game where everybody has a clear awareness of how his work impacts the numbers.

A Furniture Dealer's Testament

Imagine being worth a reported $30 billion and counting every penny like it was your last. Welcome to the world of Ingvar Kamprad, the founder of Swedish furniture retailer IKEA. His original simple business proposition was to bring affordable, well-designed furniture to the masses, people he refers to as the "many." And he's doing it with stunning success.

Kamprad's dedication and focus to IKEA's BIG objective manifested itself in a document he wrote in December 1976, entitled *A Furniture Dealer's Testament.* In it, he stated that "All nations and societies in both the East and the West spend a disproportionate amount of their resources on satisfying a minority of the population. In our line of business, for example, far too many of the fine designs and new ideas are reserved for a small circle of the affluent." Kamprad's business objective for IKEA grew out of that simple observation.

Like The Warehouse's Tindall, Ingvar Kamprad is a man of the people. His idea of a luxury vacation is riding his bike. He refuses to fly first class and, even though retired, he still visits IKEA stores to keep a feel for where the business really happens: in the store. Today, the world's only global furniture brand achieves sales per employee sales 50 percent greater than the industry average.

The son of farmers in northern Sweden, Kamprad had a modest upbringing. While in his teens he started importing small items like ballpoint pens and selling them for a modest profit. Tired of wasting money on middlemen to import, distribute and handle his goods, he eventually decided to import himself.

From belt buckles, pens and watches, Kamprad moved to furniture and as furniture sales continued to grow he began to experience a worrisomely high percentage of furniture damaged in transport—broken table legs, that type of thing. The European insurance companies were beginning to grumble.

One day in 1952, Kamprad's trusted jack-of-all-trades, Gillis Lundgren, came up with the idea that changed the furniture industry forever: "God, what a lot of space it takes up. Let's take the legs off and put them under the tabletop."

The rest is history. IKEA's flat-pack methodology rocketed them past the competition. "After that [table] followed a whole series of other self-assembled furniture, and by 1956 the concept was more or less systematized," writes Kamprad. "The more 'knockdown' we could produce, the less damage occurred during transport and the lower freight costs were."

And that value was passed on to IKEA's customers.

Driving him the entire time was his commitment to providing high-quality, affordable, stylish items to ordinary people. He recalls with distaste when he visited Italy and saw firsthand whom the "well-designed" furniture had been reaching. "I had an awakening," he writes, "when I went to the Milan Fair and visited a large carpet supplier. Thanks to him, I was able to see ordinary Italian households, the homes of simple clerks and workers. What I saw surprised me: heavy, dark furniture; a single lightbulb above a heavy dining-room table; a chasm between all the elegance at the fair and what could be seen in the homes of ordinary people."

Kamprad has always thought that it was laziness that created expensive furniture design solutions. "Any architect can design a desk that will cost 5000 kronor," he writes in *A Furniture Dealer's Testament*. "But only the most highly skilled can design a good, functional desk that will cost 100 kronor. Expensive solutions to any kind of problem are usually the work of mediocrity."

Even though Kamprad no longer actively manages IKEA, his legacy, in documents like *A Furniture Dealer's Testament,* lives on. IKEA employees still refer to him as if he were actively managing the company. His BIG objective—affordable well-designed furniture for the *many*—has been so influential that it's outgrown his presence at the company and will most likely outlive him.

How many furniture retailers, or retailers *period*, out there think like Ingvar, and have such a fervent commitment to their BIG objective? According to our research . . . none!

Focus

Most people in business are only too familiar with the rants of the beleaguered CEO, general manager, sales manager or plant manager out to cover his own butt, who harrumphs, "The only thing that matters for the next quarter is maximizing profit" . . . or new business . . . or productivity . . . or whatever. And then proceeds to create an initiative with a lofty project name like PUFF—People United For Our Factory. The next quarter, of course, management is back again with another equally preposterous set of initials asking people to be or do something different. Most workers have been asked to focus and refocus on so many phony-baloney programs so many times by so many people that it's no wonder they become cynical.

To focus means to concentrate attention or effort. Unfortunately, most corporate leaders act as though they suffer from attention deficit disorder when it comes to keeping their companies focused on mastering a simple BIG objective.

This lack of clarity inevitably leads to that same old stuff every corporate employee has witnessed too many times: an inability to move quickly, hidden agendas, unhappy workers, turf wars, finger pointing, a constant need for phalanxes of outside consultants to try and sort things out, palace intrigue and eventually a CYA mentality. It's tough to be productive when there's a swamp full of superfluous man-made issues to wade through each day.

Think about how Kmart ended up in bankruptcy court because of its inability to focus on a simple BIG objective. One day, former CEO Charles Conaway directs his company to underprice Wal-Mart on thirty thousand staple items, even though Wal-Mart can't be bested in that category. When that doesn't work, he proudly proclaims his store to be "the authority for moms, home and kids," and proceeds to enlist the edgy Spike Lee to direct Kmart's next advertising campaign. Duh! Any organization that complicates things with too many man-made issues will eventually lack clarity of purpose.

We knew our observation that companies begin their journey to productivity with an across-the-board adoption of a simple BIG objective was significant. But it turned out an even larger lesson awaited.

Once a company's people have successfully developed and demonstrated their ability to master a simple BIG objective, it appears that their new skill set allows them to begin focusing on other BIG objectives as well. Yet there's an important caveat here. People can successfully focus on two or more objectives just as effectively as when they are focusing on only one, *provided the new BIG objective or objectives are layered on or build upon the initial objective*.

For example, once Lantech had mastered the art of productivity on the factory floor, they discovered it took the company a full week to enter an order for a machine they were able to build in just eleven hours. By focusing on order entry while maintaining productivity on the factory floor, they were able to reduce entry time to minutes. Next, they realized that even with a score of accountants they weren't getting a monthly financial statement until the twenty-fifth of the following month. That became an additional focus. According to CFO Jean Cunningham, the financial statement is now ready on the first day of the month, produced by an accounting staff one-third its previous size.

At SRC, once Jack Stack had taught everyone the basics of business, it was a natural progression to begin making the company more productive through the improvement of every line on the financial statement. As Stack says, "In twenty years we've had more than twenty different bonus programs, each based on what we needed to be doing to become more efficient and profitable." But he cautions, "We've only been able to have all those different bonus programs because everyone understands business."

Soon after Bill Zollars's proclamation that Yellow would no longer be a freight company but a service business, it became obvious, he says, that his lily-white, male-dominated company needed to diversify, and that became another objective to focus upon.

As long as additional objectives are understood by everyone as complementing or adding to the original simple BIG objective, the workplace won't become confused by mixed messages and signals.

Where Does It Come From?

How do leaders and managers go about developing a simple BIG objective that will allow them to focus the efforts of everyone in their store, department, division or company?

In all the companies we studied, the objective was born from a defining moment in the life of the person leading the effort. The same thing applies whether the leader is the CEO transforming her company, the production manager transforming the factory floor, the sales manager building a new team or the small business owner resurrecting a retail store. The simple BIG objective never comes from accounting, human resources or a centralized department of strategic planning, and it has nothing to do with the current quarter's profit numbers or the CEO's current hot button.

Pat Lancaster's defining moment came the day he lost his battle for patent protection before the Supreme Court. He could have sold the company, cashed in his chips and spent the rest of his years chasing the sun. Instead he chose to *create the world's most productive factory*.

Jack Stack's defining moment came with the sudden realization that with an 89 to 1 debt-to-capital ratio, there was only a slim chance his company would exist for long. He chose to *teach everyone business*.

The death knells were ringing for Yellow Corp. when Bill Zollars stepped to the plate and said, "This company is going to be rebuilt on the kinds of customer service attitudes that made Starbucks so great."

All the companies we studied began their journey into productivity by adopting a simple BIG objective. It doesn't seem to matter what it is . . . only that one exists, that it's authentic, and that it fundamentally impacts the way business is done. Sun Microsystems CEO Scott McNeely says it this way: "If you put enough wood behind the arrow, it will hit the target."

So what's the defining moment that's going to allow you to develop a simple BIG objective to serve as the strategy for driving your business, division or company to become more productive? And once you have it, how will you move it through the organization and have everyone believe and rally behind the quest for building a more productive enterprise? Read on.

2

The Hard Work Begins

The first job of a leader or manager is to crystallize for people where the business is going and how it's going to get there.

—Ken Iverson, former CEO, Nucor

When an illusionist performs a mind-boggling feat of magic, it leaves us wondering, "How in the heck did he do that?"

Magic is fun to watch; by the end of the performance everyone is delighted to have been so thoroughly and amusingly fooled. David Copperfield didn't really make the Statute of Liberty disappear and Roy didn't actually turn Siegfried into a tiger.

People know from the get-go that magic isn't real.

But lots of business managers and leaders—the same ones who would chortle that "of course magic isn't real"—spend precious time searching for magical answers on how to improve productivity and actually end up damaging (sometimes even fatally wounding) their credibility and their business.

In business, magical solutions don't exist. If you want to drive your business into becoming more productive, you'll need a willingness to face tough realities and make tough decisions. You will need the guts to confront every significant problem and stick to the BIG objective like glue despite the pleas and crying from the people who fear change.

Why People Don't Get Onboard

There are lots of reasons why workers become cynical and don't seem eager to climb aboard management-driven initiatives. If you accept the premise that most people have at some time suffered from overly high expectations that resulted in disappointment, it's easy to understand the reluctance to adopt the next new thing from management. As employees see it, they've been promised, they've believed and they've been disappointed too many times. No wonder they resist efforts to focus on another new initiative.

Over the past couple of decades, millions of managers have trotted off for a promised *company transforming and life-changing seminar* based on the latest management magic. Remember MBO, matrix, zero-based budgeting, management by wandering around, one-minute management, theory Z and the scores of others? Afterward managers returned to their desks starry-eyed and made big backslapping pronouncements to have everyone join them in *embracing* the new future.

And again the troops, who had been through the drill countless times, smirked, exchanged knowing smiles and wondered how long they'd have to wait it out. They knew it wouldn't be too long before they'd be asked to embrace (isn't that a better word for the bedroom?) yet another management indulgence.

No one likes being manipulated. And unfortunately the introduction of all the alphabet-soup management systems, even the ones of real value, carries an unspoken message. "We're the bosses; you're just the workers. We know what's right and you don't. And now we have a new system to get production up and whip *your* sorry butts into shape." Introductions of new systems, one after another, become a giant pain in the neck. And so resistance to change, a natural protective device of humans, becomes fortified.

Most people see right through these kinds of exhortations from business owners, CEOs, department heads and managers. They see these statements as self-serving, manipulative and filled with empty words that offer no payoff for them.

But merely having a simple BIG objective won't do anything toward building a more productive organization unless you're prepared to courageously do whatever is required to move the idea throughout the organization.

Unless the BIG objective is genuine and authentic, people won't believe it and every effort toward making the business unit more productive will be thwarted.

When the simple BIG objective is as authentic as that of Stephen Tindall (The Warehouse), Jack Stack (SRC), Pat Lancaster (Lantech), Herb and Marion Sandler (World Savings), Bill Zollars (Yellow Corp.), Ingvar Kamprad (IKEA), Dan DiMicco (Nucor), and Michael O'Leary (Ryanair), then you have a valid starting point for beginning to build an incredibly productive company. That's when the really hard work begins.

The Down and Dirty on Getting It Done

During our research we uncovered six tactics used by the leaders of productive organizations to sell and move the BIG idea (strategy) through their organizations. These six tactics work whether you're managing a team of engineers, directing a sales force, running a burger joint or commanding a *Fortune* 500 company. Each results in the enterprise becoming focused, which is a requirement of productivity.

1. Live it

The folks who lead, manage and work in some of the world's most productive enterprises turned out to be, in every instance, modest people, without any of the Enron excesses of privilege. They are completely committed to the achievement of their BIG objective, to the welfare of the people within their organizations and to living lives that can best be described as unpretentious.

In Springfield, Missouri, as I toured around with SRC's Jack Stack in his mud-splattered Ford pickup, visiting the SRC manufacturing facilities scattered around town, he mused about his role. "For me, it's simple. People either get it or they don't. They either know how business works and how to make themselves into a revenue-generating product or they don't. As I look around the world, I see too much suffering and I know my mission is to teach people how to play the game of business. I used to build trucks and at the end of the day I'd see a fifty-ton truck come off the line. Then I built engines and I'd watch them come off the line. Now my only job is to teach people how to become productive businesspeople." He summed up with what for him is the bottom line: "It's the reason I exist."

Dan DiMicco, the CEO of Nucor and an affable storyteller, explains his company's commitment to living what it believes by offering what he calls "a story we've told at Nucor for years that sums up the way we feel about managing and leading our business."

The story is this: "There's a chicken and a pig sitting in a bar talking about things, trying to outdo each other. Finally they get on the subject of commitment. With their beers in front of them, the chicken clucks and says, 'I know the true meaning of commitment. Every day I'm committed to putting eggs on the table for breakfast.' The pig chokes on his beer, spits it all over the chicken and blurts, 'You don't even know the meaning of commitment. When my bacon is sitting next to those eggs, I'm really committed.'"

Nucor, America's largest steelmaker in terms of both tons produced and profits, is a fascinating company with an early history that held few clues about its becoming arguably the most productive company in the world.

The first seventy years of the company's existence were filled with as many coughs and hiccups as one can imagine. Launched in 1904 as the second car-making venture of Ransom Olds, the man who founded Oldsmobile, the company stopped making cars in 1936 and finally sold its truck-manufacturing operations in 1957. After bankruptcies, false starts and missed opportunities, Nucor merged in 1955 with another company to form Nuclear Corporation of America. Nuclear then purchased Vulcraft, a maker of steel joists, an acquisition notable only because with the company came its manager, Ken Iverson. In 1965, when the parent company was bleeding money and near bankruptcy again, the board of directors turned over the CEO reins to Iverson.

He quickly shut down or sold half the company's businesses, focused its operation solely on the production of steel joists and, because of a reliance on imported steel for the company's needs, in short order moved into the business of making steel.

From the time Iverson took over the company until now, the firm has never laid off an employee, pays its workers 30 to 40 percent more than the industry average, has had 132 successive quarters of profitability and has driven the time it takes to produce a ton of steel from ten hours in the 1980s to less than one today.

While Nucor has been hitting one home run after another, the steel industry itself has been going into the Dumpster. Since 1998, forty American steel companies have fallen into bankruptcy. Of the fourteen steel companies followed by Standard & Poor's, only one, Nucor, is healthy. The bonds of eleven of the fourteen are rated as junk, ten have negative outlooks and another hangs perilously close to default.

Even though he handed over the CEO job to a handpicked successor in 1996, the presence of Iverson (who passed away in April 2002) continues to loom larger than life at Nucor headquarters. His portrait graces the reception area of the firm's very modest corporate headquarters; his name is invoked in nearly every conversation as though people wonder, "What would Ken do?" It's as if he has become the personal mentor of every person who works at the company; his presence felt in every decision.

As I began my first interview with Dan DiMicco, the current CEO, he became almost frighteningly quiet, stared me straight in the eyes, paused and said, "I don't want you writing anything about this company without taking into account the legacy of the founding leaders. I don't want you *not* to have that perspective when you're doing your book."

Like the leaders of other productive companies, Ken Iverson also led with a simple BIG objective, one easily understood by every employee and one that continues to drive the company today even in his absence. Although Iverson's education was in aeronautical and mechanical engineering, hardly touchy-feely fields of study, he knew that others in the company wanted the same things he did. "We'll build a company," he told them, "where people will earn according to their productivity, will have a job tomorrow if they do it properly today and a company where everyone will be treated fairly." Those words constituted the BIG objective that Iverson laid out to his workers and because he believed them and lived them, they believed him and produced.

DiMicco was obviously a good student. Also schooled as an engineer, he expresses his take on Iverson's words this way: "You have to live what you say. If you say it, you better do it. Not partway, not halfway, not three-quarters way, but all the way, all the time." On his office door hangs a picture of Yoda from *Star Wars*, with his famous line, "There is no try. There is only do."

The moment the manager or leader professes a BIG objective but is busted by the employees—caught engaging in conduct contrary to the objective—his credibility is gone and he'd better be prepared to either personally apologize to everyone in the organization and ask for one more chance . . . or pack his bags and leave.

2. Sell It

Every manager, boss and leader needs to understand that their first responsibility is to sell the BIG idea throughout the entire company. Those who don't understand that are unfit for the jobs they hold.

Bill Zollars of Yellow says, "The only way for me to start the ball rolling was to get in front of people on a face-to-face basis, one on one. During my first twelve months, I spent eighty percent of my time in the field doing town meetings. I had the following message: 'We are going to transform this company into a service business and we're going to do it by diversifying our workforce and having everyone work together as a team.'"

When Zollars says that he'd often do seven or eight of these meetings a day, Gregory Reid, the company's senior vice president and chief marketing officer, rolls his eyes, smiles and interrupts. "Normally I don't contradict the boss," he says, "but this time I will. Bill never did seven or eight meetings a day. It was more like a dozen to fifteen every single day."

Reid relates that he and Zollars would start each day at seven in the morning with the drivers, then do the docks and go nonstop, one meeting after another, until well past ten o'clock at night. "Wherever we could scrounge up a few people, we'd gather them together and do the pitch. Then we'd jump on a plane and repeat the exercise the next day and the next. We did it for a year."

Nucor's Dan DiMicco enthusiastically does the same thing. "When I became CEO of this company," he says emphatically, "the first thing I did was visit every division and talk with every employee I could get hold of. Some of the meetings were one person at a time, some two hundred, and all we talked about were the core values of Nucor

and how we couldn't lose focus. One of the things I promised everyone is they'd see me at least once a year and that's not easy with
thirty-five different plants, but it's absolutely imperative that I honor
my word and be there."

Some bosses think you only have to sell the BIG objective once.
"Wrong," bellows DiMicco. "It's about building a culture. How in the
hell can you do that without constantly communicating who you are,
what you stand for and where you're headed?" He insists, "It's a nonstop process. Some people forget, others head off course and we all
make mistakes. Everyone needs to keep coming back and be told
why we exist."

3. Deal with the Unions and Cynics . . . Then Move On

If I had a nickel for every time someone's told me over the years,
"You just don't understand, we're a union company and we can't
do the same things that nonunion firms do," my piggy bank would
be full.

After researching the companies selected to be in this book, I have
two observations about the issue of unionization. Those few executives who say they can't get *anything* done because of unions must
truly be uninspiring leaders. It's easy to understand why workers led
by such people require unions. And it's equally easy to understand
why highly productive companies with *genuine* cultures—like Nucor,
IKEA, World Savings, Lantech, SRC and The Warehouse—have
never become union shops.

The turnaround at Yellow is a good example of how inspired leadership can get union employees involved in sharing the BIG objective. Bill Zollars told me he had noticed no difference between
nonunion employees and those who are organized.

"All you have to do," said Zollars, "is go to the union leadership,
explain what you're doing and ask them to get on board. If what
you're talking about is genuine and authentic, they're only too happy

to go along. I explained to them that if we didn't transform ourselves into a service business, we'd be out of business. But if we succeeded, there would be even more union jobs in the future. We noticed absolutely no difference in the buy in between our union and non-union workers."

In all the companies where a turnaround was required, employee buy in took some time to achieve. The fact that it takes time means that the leadership must work relentlessly to make it happen.

Zollars says, "The first time we talked to people, maybe we got ten percent on our side. We just kept going back with the same single consistent message. Then the number grew to fifteen percent and then twenty-five percent. When you get over fifty percent you've got critical mass on your side and as new people come into the company, they buy in to the new culture."

Jack Stack of SRC admits, "Even today, after twenty years, we have a few people with chips on their shoulders. They just want to come to work every day, do their job, nothing more and nothing less. It's okay to have a few people like that, you just can't afford to have too many. We hire several hundred new people a year, and we've created such a culture, and it's so embedded, that it would be very hard not to become part of it."

Lars Nyberg, the CEO responsible for masterminding and implementing the remarkable turnaround of NCR (formerly National Cash Register) says there's no way to turn around a business or hope to make it productive without getting allies on your side. "The good news," he says, "is that in any organization, even one with a culture like this company had, there are always people who are willing to change. You need to find them and bet on them."

4. Fire Some People

Jack Stack is probably correct in his assessment: a business that's successfully moved the BIG objective through the organization, and created a suitable culture, may have room for a few cynical workers. But there's no room for them in the ranks of management. Any company that's serious about embarking on a journey to being more productive can ill afford to have cynics, naysayers and nonbelievers among its executives and managers.

Once the boss has determined the strategic BIG objective and explained it and sold it to the key players within the organization, an opportunity arises for quick, decisive action. Any boss—whether a small-business owner, a department manager or a CEO of a *Fortune* 500 company—must stay tuned to who understands and supports the BIG objective (often referred to as "it") and who doesn't. And then move without hesitation.

Within two months of assuming his turnaround role at Yellow, Bill Zollars had developed the BIG objective, started selling it to the company's workers and evaluated the key executives. On a Monday morning, referred to around the company ever since as Black Monday, Zollars fired eleven corporate officers, half the top executives in the firm.

"They weren't bad people," says Zollars. "Some of them were very talented, but they didn't get 'it' and they weren't going to get us to where we needed to go."

Bill Zollars is a friendly and immediately likable guy. A former football star for the University of Minnesota, he's comfortable without a tie, seems more like a teddy bear than a hard-nosed CEO and is routinely greeted with affection and delight by those around him. I wondered whether lopping off eleven heads in a day was tough for him to do.

"Not really," he responded. "I had some people threaten me, others crying and telling me I was all wrong, others trying to talk me out of it." It was, he admits, uncomfortable for the moment, but "once I realized that we had a house on fire and these folks weren't capable of dousing the flames, it was ultimately fairer to them and everyone who remained to have them gone, immediately!"

Dan DiMicco shares the same view. "So many leaders in business postulate that people are their most important resource. At Nucor we see it another way. We believe that the *right* people are the most important resource because they make up our culture. It's not people *per se*, but those who are eager to do things our way, who we want here and who we value."

Each of the heads of the companies we researched agreed that as the BIG objective becomes the culture they need to subscribe to these two principles: to build a more productive organization, you should not retain people who actively work against the effort. And time does *not* cure all problems; you're deluding yourself by believing the problem people will change if only given enough time. One executive who admits learning this lesson in a particularly painful way was Gil Amelio during the time he was CEO of Apple Computer. He recounts the story in his book on the experience, *On the Firing Line.*

In response to the question "How long would an executive last who didn't agree with where your organization was headed?" the answers ranged from days to minutes. No executive in these top-productivity companies said they'd give a key player months or even weeks to decide to get with the program.

5. Abandon

One of the first observations we made in studying productive companies is that, unlike their unproductive rivals, they've institutionalized the art and science of weeding out anything that would take focus off the BIG objective. They readily abandon products, processes and profit centers that might take their eye off the ball.

One of the best examples of abandonment, recounted in a Stanford

Graduate School of Business case study (2001), is the story of telecom giant Nokia's transformation from an unwieldy conglomerate of unrelated businesses into a dynamic, focused industry leader.

Originally founded in 1865 as a wood pulp mill in southern Finland, by the early 1990s the company found itself in need of outside financial investment. The new CEO, Jorma Ollila, took twenty-five key people to a retreat deep in the woods and asked only three questions: What do we do with a business portfolio that includes everything from companies building power generators to tires? How do we get the operational thing right? What sort of company can we create in terms of values?

Shortly after the retreat one of his lieutenants asked Ollila what he was going to do with Nokia. Ollila responded with a question. "How about if we start building a telecom company?" Several months later Ollila scribbled four words on a transparency and the Nokia that the world now knows was born. The words were "Focused," "Global," "Telecom" and "Value-added."

Those four words provided the focus that allowed Nokia to become one of the most productive companies in the world. In a business where basic mobile phones are increasingly becoming a commodity, Nokia keeps on adding value and reinventing them while simultaneously achieving sales per employee 40 percent more than the industry average and routinely achieving a 20 percent return on assets. Meanwhile, Nokia's competitors continually lose money.

The board gave Ollila authority to divest everything that wasn't telecom related and the company immediately sold off its power business followed shortly by tires, cables and television. According to Nokia executive Pekka Ala-Pietilä, "We weren't getting out of weak or bad businesses. We spun off businesses that were profitable. Many were profit engines," he adds, "where we had great market share, where we were global. But they weren't telecom."

Company managers at Nokia unanimously agree that having a focused BIG objective was good for morale. Said one, "Suddenly there was a strong will about where we were going and as we reflected and sprinkled that throughout the organization, it gave people energy and enthusiasm."

Contrast Nokia's ability to abandon yesterday's breadwinner with General Motors' waste of billions of dollars in an attempt to make the factories that produce Oldsmobile more productive. All while it was trying, not very successfully, to convince the American public that "It's not your father's Oldsmobile."

At the height of Apple Computer's popularity, Steve Jobs decreed that the company would never abandon its distribution system, while Michael Dell was wondering, "Why in the hell do you need a distribution system?" But Jobs has also shown focus in other areas. After returning to the helm of Apple in 1997, he abandoned the company's industry-leading PDA product, the Newton, just as it was starting to generate positive cash flow, in order to keep everyone focused on the Macintoshes and PowerBooks that are Apple's lifeblood.

Ego, avarice and greed seem to blind many managers and executives to the basic wisdom that these other executives have grasped: a company can't be productive if it tries to focus on too many things simultaneously. The attempt defies the definition of "focus."

6. Prove You're in for the Long Haul

Research consultant and bestselling author Gary Hamel has observed that typical corporate executives spend only 2.4 percent of their time actively thinking about the future. Most leaders are so busy dealing with "today stuff" and putting out fires that they don't take time to think about where the company needs to be going. They reason that with only twenty-four hours in a day, everyone needs to focus on achieving this month's numbers and this quarter's targets. A strong focus on the short term can make a company appear to be going somewhere. Managers feel good when the myriad promises they made to their higher-ups can be achieved. They're proud of jumping in with their direct reports and employees to get the work done. Leaders simply don't make time for what most consider to be sitting around pondering their navels.

But in fact there's a downside to staying in the tactical mode 100 percent of the time. An exclusively short-term focus by company leaders will come back to bite them you know where. The leader must never forget his role as visionary. Just remember that there's a huge distinction between *thinking* about the future and *focusing* on the long term.

The same intense pressure every company feels to perform *this week, month and quarter* exists at the world's most productive companies. What things are the leaders of these companies doing differently? The difference, I discovered, is that these company chieftains solve short-term issues by taking a long-term view.

Dan DiMicco of Nucor is passionate about the short-term-versus-long-term issue. "The first thing I would tell people about the culture at Nucor is that we have a long-term focus on everything. When you have a long-term focus, you interact differently in everything you do." Leaders like DiMicco exude a level of confidence and assurance that can only come from a long-term perspective.

When all decisions are based on only the short term, the results are predictable: people become dispensable ("If he doesn't pull his thumb out, get someone else who can do it"), vendors are ruthlessly pitted against one another ("I want a better price, I want it now, or you're dead meat") and the name of the game becomes getting today's job done ("I don't care how you do it, just get it done!").

"A" players don't join or stay on teams that don't have a commitment to the long term. Nobody you'd want to keep around would be willing to commit to the BIG objective of a company that exists only for the short term. Employees want to know that while they focus on the todays, their leaders are concentrating on the tomorrows. The unspoken message is sent to everyone that "Our company will be around well into the future and so it is one worth investing in and working for." Even customers rapidly sense and respond to this powerful mix of today and tomorrow.

Workers are comfortable and willing to commit themselves to a business and a BIG objective if they believe there's a future for them. Truly productive companies understand that while a business must always deliver in the short term, their real focus must be on the long term and on proving the proposition that *Less Is More* by getting everyone onboard and focused.

Ready to Become Productive?

Any businessperson truly committed to dramatically increasing productivity should follow the lead of the companies that have cracked the code on getting people onboard for the effort of achieving a BIG objective. Only when a company manages to get its people focused can it begin moving toward doing more with *less.*

Remember that everyone doesn't have to buy in. But once a sufficient number of workers are onboard with the effort and people in the organization sense a critical mass has been reached . . . then it's time to *streamline,* which is our next topic.

STREAMLINE

3

The First Tactic: The Truth

Men stumble over the truth from time to time, but most pick themselves up and hurry off as if nothing happened.

—Winston Churchill

"Come on in for a sec," goes the greeting and the voice drops to an almost conspiratorial whisper as the invitation is completed: "And *close the door* behind you."

Those must be some of the most frequently spoken words in business. What do you think comes out of all those closed-door sessions that has anything to do with making the business more productive or efficient?

Little or nothing!

Aside from a termination or business of a highly personal nature, there are typically only two things connected with business that happen behind closed doors. The most common is a conversation about who's doing what to whom—which is risky, and has no place in a productive business. The other is the sharing of highly sensitive information with someone deemed "important" enough to be in the loop.

I didn't find *any* closed doors in the world's most productive companies. (I even had trouble getting people to shut a door against intrusive noises when I wanted to tape an interview.) As a result of my research, I've concluded that the greater the number of closed doors in a company, the less likely that truthfulness and openness will be found. (You want to wager there were more closed doors around Enron than you could count?)

Truthfulness and Openness

Truthfulness—Dealing with Fact and Reality

Lantech chairman Pat Lancaster says, "When people lie, I think it means they have something to hide. Or else they don't respect the person or people they're lying to." He adds, "You can't build a productive company where trust isn't a guiding principle, and you can't have trust without truth."

As I was wrapping up my interviews at Yellow's Overland Park, Kansas, headquarters, Greg Reid, the SVP and chief marketing officer, pulled me aside to share a comment about the company's CEO. "Look," he said, "there's something you should know about Bill Zollars."

He led me behind a partition, lowered his voice and said, "I need to tell you this. Bill is the most honest man I've ever worked for in my life. He trusts people, gives them permission to do what they think is right and then guides them. That's why he's been so successful at turning Yellow Corp. into such a productive company." And he added what I thought was a bit of practical philosophy: "People only trust someone to lead them if *everything* they say is true."

The same scenarios played out over and over again at almost every company. So many people—a receptionist, a VP, a supplier, a factory worker—would pull me aside to praise the truthfulness of their company's leaders. They explained and agreed that it was *truth* that made their company such a productive place.

During my interviews with Yellow's CEO Zollars, he told me a story that perfectly captured his attitude toward dealing with truth in the business setting. He said, "I scheduled a meeting when I took over with the top eleven people in the company because I needed their read on the capabilities of the other people in the business. I had this long list of names and wanted their opinions. The first name out of the hat was this HR staffer who had been here twenty years. 'Okay, what about this guy?' I asked."

Everyone in the room stared down at their shoes, nervously cleared their collective throats and refused to say a word. Zollars had a long list of names to go through and it was beginning to look like a time-consuming and tedious day.

Finally, after a long silence, he bit the bullet. He stood up and said, "I'm not going to do this bullshit all day! So, here's what we're going to do. Steve, you're first up. If you can't give me a good reason in two sentences why you don't want this guy on your team, he's yours."

Zollars said that Steve immediately spewed like a fountain and provided a shower of reasons why the person in question wasn't capable of doing the job to get the company where it needed to go. Zollars moved on to the next name, and again no one was willing to offer an opinion. So he repeated the exercise, charging another executive with the same admonition, "Tell me why you don't want this person on your team or he's yours."

All of sudden, Zollars told me, "The floodgates opened and I heard the truth. Maybe for the first time in this company's history, there was an honest discussion about the capabilities of the key players."

Openness—That Which Isn't Locked, Closed or Blocked

A lack of openness inevitably causes gossip and rumors to spread like a California brushfire in September. A lack of openness sends crazy-making mixed messages. Instead of working to make the enterprise more productive, people spend their time climbing a ladder with their nose up the bum of the person on the rung above them trying to gain admittance to the exclusive executive club.

Closed doors distract, confuse and make everyone nervous— hardly an environment where productivity will flourish. One characteristic shared by all the once-formidable companies that have either ended up in the rubbish bin or been bitterly challenged—the Kmarts, Levitzes and Digital Equipments—is that each is or was renowned for its closed management structure.

When the cultures of highly productive companies are dissected, it appears there are three primary areas—the numbers, communication and criticism—where openness and truthfulness provide them a distinct competitive advantage in becoming more productive than their rivals.

The Numbers

Productive companies are open with all the numbers, and they score everything that's important.

In most businesses, numbers are still provided to people on a need-to-know basis. The sales manager knows the sales target, the production manager knows the costs of all the components that go into creating whatever they do and the office manager knows the costs of overhead. Then all the various departmental numbers are entered, digested and spit forth from the desktop of the CFO who, following some top secret mumbo jumbo, nervously clutches the bottom line number to his chest and hesitatingly delivers it to the top dog who sits in his office and always growls, "Nope, not good enough."

You know the drill.

Here's the real bottom line on numbers.

Conventional wisdom says the worker bees can't know how much money the business really makes because if they did, they'd all want a raise. "And besides," choke the practitioners of medieval management, "the other reason people can't have the numbers is they won't understand them anyway."

"That thinking is stupid," retorts Jack Stack of SRC. "You can only build a productive enterprise when everyone thinks like an owner. How can you ask people to think like owners if they don't know the numbers?" he asks incredulously.

"Look, we were technically upside-down with that 89 to 1 debt to equity ratio the day we bought the company. I needed to get everyone thinking like an owner. There's no way to do that unless you're completely open and everyone has access to all the numbers and understands them. Knowing them isn't enough. That's why my job was to teach everyone what debt was, what equity was and they needed to learn how to value a company. Now it's known as open book management but that's not what it is. What good are open books and having everyone know the numbers," he asks passionately, "if they don't know what in the hell the numbers mean?"

Not only will a company that keeps its numbers secret be unproductive, Stack believes, but it's actually contributing to class warfare. "Wake up and smell the coffee," he challenges. "Most of the problems the world faces are because of financial illiteracy. If you want to stop the battle between the haves and the have-nots and build productive companies, teach the have-nots what the haves know."

Jack Stack's love affair with numbers and using them to make business more productive actually started decades earlier. At nineteen, Stack says, in order to stay out of trouble, he went to work in a factory and was soon doing material scheduling. Jack's proud of the fact that he quickly became a proficient expeditor. That led to a series of management jobs, each with increasing responsibility. He was on his way.

"By the time I was in my early twenties," Stack says, "some of the people working for me were in their fifties, had been there for twenty years or more and felt they deserved my job. I had to figure out a way to get these people working with me to make the plant more productive. I promised them that if they'd help me accomplish what I needed to get done"—truthfulness again—"I'd be out of the place very soon and then they could be promoted. Then," he says, "I had to figure out how to make the place more productive.

"What's something that most people like?" he asks in a style designed to make people think with him. "America is a game-playing nation and what do you need for a game? You need a start, a finish with a score and some rules. It's damn hard to motivate assembly-line workers," he explains. "Many of them are young with no direction or goals, some are heavy drinkers who drag themselves in each morning and others have been doing it so long they just don't care.

"But whoever they are, people need to feel good about themselves every single day, and winning is a process that allows them to do that. So I decided to turn everything into a game. Technology was giving us increasing access to numbers but most managers were using them to beat people up. I was a superintendent with five hundred people working for me and all I did was run numbers all day long and turn everything into a game. We did pizza runs, turned our production lines into baseball games, bet one team against another, dressed in costumes and did whatever we needed to do to turn it into a game and let people go home a winner." And you can picture it—even the people on the losing "team" probably felt they had played the good game, and even if they hadn't, there was another one coming right up.

Continuing his story, Stack grins with remembered satisfaction. "While International Harvester was trying to figure out if putting new light fixtures on their assembly lines would motivate workers, our productivity went through the ceiling."

Imagine what a failure Stack's game playing would have been if it hadn't been predicated on keeping score. Keeping score requires that people know the numbers—how would you like to watch the Super Bowl and never know the score?

At Nucor, the approach is different but still based on sharing the truth in numbers. Everyone in the company is paid for performance. The weekly paycheck of worker Bill Smith in a Nucor plant depends on what Bill and his team produced the previous week. Openness and accuracy of numbers on an hourly, daily and weekly basis are vital in a company where everyone's compensation (including the CEO's) is based only on productivity. Steelworkers at Nucor average more than sixty thousand dollars in annual compensation with many making more than one hundred thousand dollars. By comparison, Dan DiMicco delights in pointing out that the average wage in many of the regions where Nucor's plants are located is slightly more than ten thousand dollars a year.

To illustrate the importance of openness with numbers, DiMicco told me about a Nucor acquisition of another firm. "In 2001 we made our first major acquisition as a steel company when we purchased Auburn Steel from Sumitomo. It was a solid, profitable company with good people and a good reputation, producing about four hundred thousand tons of steel a year."

DiMicco recognized they couldn't put their entire culture into place overnight, but "We did immediately implement our pay-for-productivity system, based on everyone knowing exactly what they produce. Within the first twelve months, the factory broke every record it had established in its twenty-eight-year history—including the safety record—and did it in one of the worst markets the steel industry has ever known."

At Yellow Corp., according to Bill Zollars and Greg Reid, "We had numbers up the yin-yang, but they were all fiercely protected by little departments scattered all over the place and no one seemed to know what they were or what they meant. When we decided we had

to create a service culture in order to make the company more productive, it became imperative that we measure how we were doing
and share those numbers with everyone."

Zollars adds, "When I got here and started asking about customers, all I got were blank stares. Everyone began trotting out
reams of metrics about how efficient the Yellow system was but
that's all they knew. We immediately began measuring how we were
doing with customers and sharing those numbers with everyone.
Otherwise everything I was saying would have just been empty management rhetoric."

The results of the first customer satisfaction survey were dismal,
revealing that the company disappointed customers in some way on
almost half of all deliveries. Zollars knew that Yellow couldn't improve customer satisfaction unless his people were highly motivated,
so he immediately implemented a new compensation plan whereby
a portion of everyone's paycheck, from a newly hired secretary (5
percent) to himself (80 percent), would be directly tied to customer
satisfaction. That compensation plan directly linked to Zollars's BIG
objective still remains in effect at Yellow.

In only three years Yellow managed to move from a 50 percent
satisfaction rating to the high 80s and within spitting distance of the
FedEx and UPS ratings, while dramatically increasing productivity.

It's their openness with the numbers that allowed Yellow to increase customer satisfaction, SRC to save a company and become the
most productive in their industry, and Nucor to become the most efficient steel producer in the world.

Communication

Productive companies have genuinely open communication.

Something remarkable happens throughout an organization when
the people at the top decide to be absolutely open and truthful in

their communication. They soon realize that the people who work for them aren't stupid and indeed have extraordinary contributions to make. In fact, in productive enterprises, the tactical plans to successfully achieve the BIG objective don't come from the ivory tower; the people who are closest to where the action takes place plan the best tactics.

Nucor has only five levels in their management structure for a workforce almost ten thousand strong: workers in the mills; team supervisors; plant managers; executive vice presidents to whom groups of mills report; and company CEO Dan DiMicco. "We don't have bureaucrats to manage our communication. Every employee in the company has the right to call me," says DiMicco. Then he adds, "And they do."

It's a principle he's clearly committed to: "I answer my own telephone and return every call to every employee. We urge people to go to their supervisor or plant manager first, because, as we point out, they'd want the same courtesy extended to them. But everyone—including someone newly hired—has the absolute right to call me. And when someone calls me, everyone hears about it because they tell everyone that the system actually works."

SRC's Jack Stack says one question from a worker led to a virtual transformation of the company. "As we began sharing all the numbers with everyone," he tells me, "it quickly became a beautiful place to be. Most executives are afraid that if you have completely open communication, you're going to have people complaining about needing a new machine tool to be more productive or wondering why we're always breaking down or telling management they aren't being treated like a person. But that's not what happened. The more we kept pushing people out of the box, the harder they pushed us forward."

Stack was holding one of his weekly business education sessions and reviewing all the numbers for the week when one of the workers raised his hand. "Jack," he said, "our stock is doing really well and some people are cashing out. I don't want to just be a connecting rod for them. Where's the money going to come from when *I* want to cash out?" The question struck Stack like a bolt of lightning because of the timing: it came just after he'd heard a story from a friend about a fireworks company in China.

This friend had recently visited a small village in China that is a huge center for the manufacture of fireworks. He told Stack that he was struck by finding the production being done in small, individual huts instead of a mammoth manufacturing facility. Concluding that it must be a terribly inefficient way to manufacture huge amounts of fireworks, he asked and learned the reason.

An occupational hazard of the fireworks industry is the occasional explosion. The clever people in the town had learned the hard way that if you have an explosion in a big factory, you're out of business, but if you have an explosion in one small hut, you grieve with the widow and then everyone gets back to work.

Because of one incisive tactical question from a worker who had learned to think in business terms, Stack was forced into coming up with an appropriate answer. Suddenly the story of the Chinese fireworks factory struck a chord. His answer? The way for the company to ensure there'd be money for people when they cashed out or retired, he told them, was by making the company bulletproof. Instead of one big company, they'd build lots of little companies and they'd continually evaluate them from the perspective of a potential purchaser.

Stack and his workers shifted gears a bit and soon, in addition to teaching his people about business, he began to teach them how to evaluate their business from the perspective of a potential purchaser. "We had to make certain there would always be money for everyone when they decided to cash out or retire. That's a powerful business concept and it came in the form of a question from someone who might never have been motivated to think in these terms."

SRC has started a total of thirty-nine different businesses. "A few," Stack chuckles, "didn't work out." For example, the company was probably way off base trying to open a restaurant. SRC today has twenty-two separate businesses spread across Springfield, Missouri, and its employees weekly review the performance of each in terms of how much someone would be willing to pay for it.

SRC became bulletproof as a result of management listening to and respecting its people. Valuing tactical ideas or questions from people down the line is another typical pattern of highly successful companies.

Supplier Communication

Truly open communication at productive companies isn't confined within the company but extended to suppliers and customers as well. One of the misplaced macho holdovers in a lot of businesses is the adversarial relationship they maintain with vendors and suppliers. Many seem to think they're being savvy businesspeople when they beat up vendors and suppliers on every issue ranging from price to delivery to returns. That prehistoric approach isn't what we found in productive companies where vendors are treated with respect and encouraged to think of themselves as part of the team.

That's not to suggest productive companies are touchy-feely places where the buyers roll over, play dead and pay any price. Instead, we observed complete openness with their suppliers where the mutually understood rule is, "Here's the margin we're going to make when we sell a product to our customers. We'd like to do business with you. Let's work together to figure out how you can help us sell our product at the margin we need, while allowing you to make the margin you need."

The Warehouse has teams of people who go out and work with suppliers to help each of them improve their own production, scheduling, logistics and pricing. The openness between suppliers and The Warehouse is genuine and simple, says Stephen Tindall. "We go inside their businesses and tell them we want to help them be more efficient so we can be more efficient." Tindall cites an example: suppliers that formerly shipped hundreds of orders to individual stores now ship to a central Warehouse distribution facility, resulting in significant cost savings and higher margins for both parties.

IKEA follows the same kind of thinking. According to Kent Nordin, who serves as a country manager, currently running their Australian operation, "We work on a completely integrated basis with all our suppliers and it's always on a long-term basis. It's never about the first batch of ten thousand chairs. It's for five hundred thousand chairs over the next five years."

IKEA actually invests in the business operations of its suppliers. Nordin relates the story of one of the company's major suppliers, a Romanian company. "There was a very progressive man running a government factory there," he says, "who was fired because of his innovative thinking. So we entered into a joint venture with him and we financed his machinery.

"Because we took the time to nurture and develop this supplier," says Nordin, "we now reap substantial rewards and have outstanding production. This is typical of how IKEA works."

Another example is Ireland's Ryanair, which within only a few years has become Europe's largest and most successful discount airline. Michael O'Leary, its feisty and flamboyant CEO, is very clear about being ruthlessly open and honest with customers. "We have a simple proposition at Ryanair," he says. "We'll fly you where you want to go, we'll do it cheaper than anyone else and we'll do it in safe airplanes. But there's nothing else. If someone wants a coffee or a cola on board, they buy it. It's about cheap safe seats, period!"

Walking through a gigantic IKEA store, customers can't help but notice the placards and signs everywhere reminding them to pick up a telephone to ask a question, go to a kiosk to place their order, walk this way to do that and always return their cart—so prices can stay low. By being honest, forthright and open with his customers, a Harvard Business School case study concluded, "Ingvar Kamprad made his customers his partners; low prices in exchange for serving yourself, taking it away and assembling it yourself."

Contrast that attitude against a typical current unspoken business and advertising tactic used by many companies to get customers—"Promise everything and deliver nothing." This practice is best illustrated by a short story.

On the ride to heaven a consumer is informed he'll have the opportunity of sampling both heaven and hell before deciding where he wants to reside for time immemorial. A bit nervous but wanting to get it over with, he decides to sample hell first. After a long elevator ride down, he is greeted by a friendly guy in a tuxedo. Before him is a vast hall filled with great music, a nonstop party, wonderful food and booze, and all his friends who have gone before him. Reminded after a while that it's time to sample heaven, he gets back on the elevator and up he goes.

Upon arrival in heaven there are lots of little angel wings and soft harp music but no party. Frankly, it suffers in contrast. After floating on a puffy white cloud for a while he's approached by Saint Peter, who asks if he's made a decision. "Yeah, I have. No offense to you, Pete, but this place is pretty boring. I think I'll pick hell."

With a click of his saintly fingers our consumer finds himself back in hell but this time a nasty-looking Lucifer with horns, tail and pitchfork greets him and he's surrounded by ranting and wailing people boiling in cauldrons.

"Hey, what's up?" he asks. "This isn't the hell I remember!"

"That's right, it's not," grins the devil. "The last time you were here you were a prospect. Now you're a customer!" *

If IKEA, The Warehouse, Ryanair and the other companies whose productivity dramatically exceeds that of their rivals weren't open and truthful with their customers, there's no chance their customers would be so fiercely loyal.

Criticism

At productive companies, *process* is criticized—not people.

"Process" is a term (for those of you lucky enough to have missed it) that came into vogue in many business circles during the past decade. Originally intended as a method of giving voice to and receiving input from all "employee stakeholders," somewhere during its journey through most companies it got shanghaied by the do-nothing Commie types who were incapable of designing, building, selling or servicing anything so that the only valid contribution they could make was their ability (in their own minds) to "process" stuff.

Before long companies were processing everything from vision statements to bathroom breaks, from employee manuals to parking lot policies. Process requires facilitators, meeting rooms, recording secretaries, reams of paper and months of time for all the meetings required to arrive at a consensus. Meanwhile all those people processing stuff aren't designing, making or selling anything. Predictably, as managers have become fearful of the politically correct "process police," every decision in process-oriented companies slows down and nothing becomes more productive.

Warning: The ultimate objective of the process police is to turn

---

*There are few things I dislike more than having someone use my original material without acknowledging the source. Since first hearing this story several years ago I've spent many hours trying to find the original source, to no avail. I offer my thanks and sincere apologies to the author.

once-successful companies into giant town hall meetings. (They love hearing themselves talk.)

People at highly productive companies share a disdain for companies whose culture is based on processing everything. The ones that talk instead of doing have become a big joke. Productive companies don't talk and process—they do. When something needs fixing or improving, there's no finger-pointing or blame-placing. Instead the people closest to the problem are empowered to fix the problem on the spot. If it's a sales problem, a bunch of sales types are chosen to huddle together and figure out what to do. If it's a production problem, people on the line are authorized to shut down the line, define the problem, fix it and get it going again. If it's an MIS problem, the folks with pocket protectors get together, make the appropriate decision, fix it and then go back as fast as they can to supporting the people who produce the company's goods. The approach reflects the company's choice of action instead of talk.

Jean Cunningham, CFO at Lantech, argues persuasively that if a company wants to improve productivity, its people should transform the organization into an action-oriented mind-set. "The reason," she says, "that so much attention has been paid to manufacturing productivity is because areas outside of manufacturing have an attitude that their work is different, somehow special, and because there's an intellectual component to what they do, that they're above the challenge of criticism and continual improvement."

People who believe that their contribution of thought and talk is more precious, more valuable, than the work of people in manufacturing, sales and operations hold a fundamentally wrong attitude that's both dangerous and destructive.

But without open communication and a valid criticizing process, Cunningham argues, "a company will be unprepared to tear down the walls and barriers, and will instead pitch that which doesn't add real value."

Organizations that are determined to be more productive must have the ability to constantly differentiate between work that adds value and work that doesn't. And work that adds clear value should be prized above all.

Some People Don't Do Truth and Openness Well

As described in the first two chapters, all the highly productive companies we studied share in common ownership of an essentially unique culture. Acknowledging that not everyone will fit their culture, most of the companies have a probationary hiring period. Without penalty, at the end of ninety days, the company can decide whether or not they want the worker. As Dan DiMicco says, "It works both ways. The worker can also decide she doesn't want the company and our culture."

Because people in productive enterprises constantly know how the company is doing financially, are scored and compensated on both individual and team productivity, and are without processes to hide behind, these cultures aren't for everyone. There are some who just can't handle the environment. It's during the first ninety days that each company hopes to shake out people who aren't a good fit.

Interestingly most of the shaking out comes from peer pressure and not from the bosses or supervisors. "When you measure and pay for productivity and have people on teams, most of the personnel issues are resolved quickly," according to DiMicco. "Other team members don't want slouches that negatively affect their weekly paycheck. If we have fifteen people on a team and made a couple of errors in hiring and end up with two bad apples, chances are good that within ninety days they'll be gone."

Once someone fully gets onboard with the company culture, the turnover is far below average. Two-thirds of Jack Stack's original three-hundred-member workforce from twenty years ago are still with SRC. Yellow turns over only 2 percent of their drivers each year and the employee turnover rates at Lantech, Ryanair, The Warehouse and IKEA are among the lowest in their respective industries.

Imagine the giant strides in productivity that any department or business can achieve by doing nothing more than emulating the first two lessons we've covered in our study of highly productive enterprises: Install a BIG strategic objective that ultimately becomes the culture. And then create an open and truthful environment where everyone knows and understands the numbers and is compensated for specific contributions.

Highly productive enterprises prove the proposition that *Less Is More* with *more* truth and *less* you-know-what.

Productivity increases even more when the enterprise is prepared to quickly dismantle unnecessary structures. That's where we're headed next.

4

Destroy the Bureaucracy and Make It Simple

The only thing that saves us from the bureaucracy is its inefficiency.
—Eugene McCarthy

While preparing to travel to Charlotte, North Carolina, for research at Nucor that would include an interview with CEO Dan DiMicco, I called to ask for a recommendation of a hotel close to their headquarters. One of the Nucor telephone operators gave me the name of a place where their visitors often stay.

Early on the morning of my meetings I called the hotel's front desk to ask how far Nucor was from the hotel. The clerk had a lovely smile in her voice as she said, "If you look out your window, sir, you'll see it just across the parking lot."

I parted the curtains and sure enough, there it was, the multistoried headquarters of Nucor, the nation's largest producer of steel. I wondered what floor the CEO's office suite was on and whether we'd be meeting in his private office or in a conference room.

At the appointed hour I strode across the parking lot, pushed open one of the double glass doors and entered the marble-floored Nucor lobby expecting dazzling stainless steel sculptures, a row of receptionists behind a long, curving, burnished reception desk and walls filled with art.

Oops! It wasn't the Nucor lobby. This entryway was standard-issue office building—no plush sofas, no security book, no badges, no smiling, streamlined receptionist. *What gives?* I wondered.

Guessing that Nucor was the major tenant and had perhaps leased out a few floors to other companies, I casually checked the building directory to find out which floor was listed for the company's main reception. I was shocked to find many other companies listed on the directory; it turned out that Nucor occupied only a single suite of offices and was one of the building's smaller tenants. Nucor, the *Fortune* 500 company? Was this possible?

I was puzzled. How in the heck could the nation's biggest steel company be managed from such small digs? *Maybe*, I thought, *their administrative center is located in another facility*.

"What the hell did you expect to find, the Taj Mahal?" boomed Dan DiMicco. He pumped my hand and welcomed me. I was in the right place, and I was stunned. My prepared words flew right out of my mind.

As we walked down a narrow hallway toward his office, DiMicco said, "Let me tell you what you'll find at Nucor. You'll find clean carpets and painted walls. That's it. You won't find any gold-plated faucets or fancy surroundings. And here at the home office," he continued, "you'll also find forty-two people. That's all."

It turned out the Nucor "telephone operator" who had provided me with the name of the hotel is Betsy. She is the receptionist, phone answering lady and highly skilled front person who has been with the company for twenty-four loyal years.

I would in time learn that DiMicco's decor decisions for the company's headquarters would apply to the home offices of all the productive companies we researched. In every case they were clean, simple and orderly. None was overstaffed with people just wandering around looking for something to do. One might easily conclude that these companies run on too few of everything rather than one extra. Nothing is done for image or comfort alone.

Spartan surroundings are a metaphor for another shared trait of successful companies: we found that each of them has a management structure as starkly simple as their home offices. Just as you don't find Oriental rugs floating over waxed and buffed wood parquet floors, neither do you find layers of bureaucratic refuse to wade through. Highly productive companies have masterminded the ability to run a large business without the typically wasteful and cumbersome bureaucracy.

Why Bureaucracy?

In most businesses, as revenues grow so does the bureaucracy.

The scenario is typical and probably familiar to you: when the person handling calls from customers seems overwhelmed, rather than considering a range of options, most companies opt for the obvious. Promote the person to become head of a newly formed "customer care" department, print some business cards, assign a budget that includes an assistant and start giving the new department "voice" at all company meetings. Ditto for HR, planning, finance, purchasing and procurement, marketing, strategy, sales, communication, IT and so on.

And before long there are enough departments and department heads for a department head holiday party, an in-house magazine (another department), travel agency (another department) and a department to coordinate and oversee all the other departments. And each department becomes a silo standing separate and apart from all the other silos. Meanwhile the public relations department (of course there's one of these by now) is issuing "See how successful we are" releases that point to the department structure as a sign of achievement.

The focus on productivity becomes blurred while the department heads measure their importance and self-worth by the size of their departments and their budgets, and jockey to get the greatest

amount of face time with the man in charge to defend the importance of their department's vital work. Maintaining and growing the
bureaucracy becomes the new company focus. The illusion is
growth; the reality is trouble ahead.

Some companies even sport names for their bureaucracies. While
Xerox continues to fight for its life, suffering one setback after another, the folks at headquarters in Stamford, Connecticut, still fondly
refer to the firm's bureaucratic structure as Burox. Highly productive
businesses, large or small, don't spend time inventing pet names for
their bureaucracies; they produce products, not bureaucracies. Leaders of these companies don't tolerate bureaucracies; when they discover one in their organization, they ruthlessly eliminate it.

"This Is Your Captain Speaking"—the Outspoken CEO

Dear Jason,

I have no interest in participating in your book. I have an abiding fear
of CEOs who either write books or participate in them. They should
run their businesses and stop pontificating about how they should be
run. Far too much of this stuff is designed to gratify the egos of CEOs
and mine is big enough already.

Michael O'Leary

CEO

Ryanair

Michael O'Leary's first letter of many to me (he was a tough nut to
crack) speaks volumes about him, the airline he runs and how, in
only twelve years, he's managed to turn a small, red-ink-gushing
start-up with a handful of turboprops and fifty-seven employees into
the world's most efficient and productive airline.

His letter was to the point—just like his airline and his BIG
objective.

Perhaps you hadn't heard about Mr. O'Leary and his airline before encountering them in these pages, but if he has his way (and he has a rich history of getting it), you'll not only hear about Ryanair, you'll be flying in their planes in the not-too-distant future. Shamelessly modeled after America's Southwest Airlines, Mr. O'Leary's airline, based in Dublin, Ireland, currently beats every other airline in the world—including Southwest—on all productivity metrics.

Ryanair flies to suburban or secondary airports, flies only one type of aircraft, has no assigned seating, doesn't commission travel agents, discounts all tickets sold and pays all its people à la Nucor: low salaries and big bonuses based on productivity. (Two-thirds of a flight attendant's compensation are based on the number of coffees, cokes and duty-free merchandise they can sell and how many flight segments they fly.)

Industrywide, the average airline worker generates $190,000 in revenues each year. While Southwest Airlines consistently beats the averages and does 10 percent more per employee than other carriers, Ryanair produces a startling $297,000 in revenue per employee per year—almost 40 percent more than the average. In terms of profit per employee, Southwest does 25 percent better than the industry average but Ryanair thrashes the competition by a mind-boggling factor of *four*. In 2001, a year in which airlines worldwide lost a collective $15 billion, Ryanair achieved a 26 percent net margin.

Days after September 11, while airlines worldwide were cutting routes and laying off hundreds of thousands of workers, O'Leary said, "I am absolutely convinced that the wrong response is to ground aircraft, fire people, offer fewer flights and sell these remaining seats at higher prices. This seems to me to be a one-way ticket to oblivion, no matter how much subsidy and how much state aid is given to loss-making, inefficient high-fare carriers."

Then he quickly plastered Europe with huge posters proclaiming LET'S FIGHT BACK, announced that his company was giving away three

hundred thousand free seats to boost consumer confidence and selling an additional one million tickets for fifteen dollars apiece while
simultaneously announcing the purchase of one hundred new Boeing jets, the largest order in European history.

Founded in 1986 as a sideline business by Tony Ryan, one of Ireland's wealthiest businessmen, Ryanair began by flying the formerly
highly regulated skies between Ireland and Britain. In its first year,
with only those fifty-seven employees, it flew five thousand passengers on its one route; four years later the fledgling carrier was flying
six hundred thousand passengers across the Irish Sea each year in
fourteen airplanes but was hemorrhaging tens of millions of dollars.
In 1991 a brash, twenty-eight-year-old Michael O'Leary joined the
company as Tony Ryan's personal assistant.

O'Leary started his career as a tax accountant, but when he bought
and quickly sold his first newsstand for a big profit he realized he
was better suited to wheeling and dealing than preparing corporate
tax forms. In a determined effort to stem the losses and figure out
how to have Ryanair survive, O'Leary traveled to the United States to
study Southwest Airlines.

Returning to Ireland, O'Leary convinced Ryan to slash the number of routes from twenty to just five, dispose of the turboprops and
slice fares on 70 percent of all available seats. By 1992 Ryanair was
flying a small fleet of six jets, its workforce numbered 350 people
and the airline eked out its first small profit. Ryanair had been reborn
as Europe's first genuine discount carrier; it may have been modeled
on Southwest but O'Leary was determined to do things even better.

In 1994, having proven himself to Ryan, O'Leary was given the
title of CEO and gifted with 25 percent of the airline's stock. And
then it was off to the races for Ryanair.

O'Leary—a man whose standard business dress is jeans, suede
shoes and a rugby jersey and whose demeanor can best be described
as bullish, brusque and brash—says his airlines BIG objective is

simple: "We're going to be Europe's biggest scheduled air carrier and do it by guaranteeing customers the lowest price and a safe flight that normally gets there on time." Then he brags, saying with 100 percent truthfulness, "But that's all they'll get. Nothing more, nothing less."

With only 1,700 employees, Ryanair carries more than ten million passengers each year, a number the company expects to triple by 2010, which would make it Europe's biggest airline. By comparison, the average airline employs eight times the number of employees of Ryanair to carry the same number of passengers.

When quizzed in a rare interview by Tom Chesshyre of *The Times* of London about why his newspaper receives more complaints concerning Ryanair's customer service than any other airline, O'Leary responded in typically bombastic style. "Listen," he said, "we care for our customers in the most fundamental way possible: we don't screw them every time we fly them." He went on to add, "I have no time for certain large airlines which say they care and screw you for six or seven hundred quid [slang for a British pound sterling] almost every time you fly."

Other than cheap airfares, customer service at Ryanair is nonexistent, O'Leary boasts. "If passengers want coffee, tea or a packet of peanuts, they can pay for them. If a plane is canceled, will we put you up in a hotel overnight? Absolutely not. If a plane is delayed, will we give you a voucher for a restaurant? Absolutely not."

When Chesshyre grilled O'Leary about the difficulties customers experience when they try to reach Ryanair, O'Leary explained the questions away. "Our position is simple," he replied. "We don't take any phone calls . . . because people keep you on the phone all bloody day. We employ four people in our customer service department. Every complaint must be in writing and we undertake to respond within twenty-four hours."

O'Leary claims that 70 percent of all customer complaints are from consumers who want a refund on a flight not taken. "Too bad," he told the reporter. "Our policy is clearly stated as being nonchangeable, nontransferable and nonrefundable." But even so, O'Leary insisted, flying Ryanair is still a good deal. "Even if they have to buy a second ticket because Granny is sick or they can't get the day off work, people will still save money."

For a man who refuses to use e-mail, calling it "garbage," it might not surprise you to learn that O'Leary canceled the company's Christmas party to boost profits, got rid of in-flight meals because "they taste like crap" and charges people applying for jobs as pilots a one-hundred-dollar application fee. He defends that practice by saying, "Look, we get thousands of applications for positions as pilots, including from bloody sixteen-year-old kids with no driver's licenses, we have to sort through. What's wrong with making them pay?"

But Ryanair has no bureaucracy.

None!

Getting Rid of the Bureaucracy

After delivering a particularly intense lecture, the late philosophy professor and author Morris Cohen was confronted by a sobbing young student who cried, "You've emptied my head of everything I've ever believed in and given me nothing to replace it with." Professor Cohen sternly replied, "One of the twelve labors of Hercules was to clean out the stables. He was not required to fill them again."

The opening pages of this chapter having, I trust, emptied the stable of any tendencies toward bureaucracy, I sense an obligation, despite the example of Hercules, to provide action suggestions— guidelines for how an organization can actually go about getting rid of bureaucracy.

Most of the companies that made the final cut for inclusion in this book were companies that were founded by people completely and unalterably opposed to bureaucracy (The Warehouse, Nucor, SRC, IKEA, World Savings), so they had never confronted dismantling one. The remaining few were businesses that had been forced by economic necessity (Lantech, Ryanair and Yellow) to decisively abandon cumbersome multilayered structures. It's amazing how fast unproductive bureaucratic structures can be dismantled when there's no money in the bank.

IKEA's solution to minimizing bureaucracy is to squelch it before it can even begin to seep into departments as the company grows. Ingvar Kamprad says, "Historical baggage, fear and unwillingness to take responsibility are the breeding ground for bureaucracy. Indecisiveness generates more statistics, more studies, more committees and more bureaucracy. Bureaucracy complicates and paralyzes!" This simply isn't a man who tolerates waste. Employees at IKEA and all other highly productive companies share the same philosophy.

Kamprad has institutionalized the destruction of complicated corporate hierarchies. Kent Nordin says, "We still have what's called 'Anti-Bureaucracy Week,'" a time when executives must leave the safe, secluded confines of their corporate offices and get down and dirty in an IKEA store for an entire week.

He continues, "For at *least* one week every year, everyone has to work in a store. And that can be anything from pushing carts to serving as a cashier, or in sales, whatever you can do."

But there's a caveat. Nordin adds, "All of the executives must be there on weekends, when the stores are the busiest, teeming with shoppers of all kinds, crying babies and arguing couples. It's not enough to check in on a Monday and out on a Thursday afternoon. You have to be there when the heat is on." Their founder created the program, Nordin explains, "because he is dead scared of bureaucracy. He is very afraid about the people who make decisions becoming out of touch."

Straight-talking CEO Bill Zollars of Yellow Corp., on the other hand, found a bumbling bureaucracy when he was recruited with the specific task of breathing life back into a lumbering giant that had fallen on hard times. Zollars agreed to reveal his eight steps for what he calls "blowing up" a bureaucracy, and allowed me to share them here.

Eight Steps for Driving a Stake Through the Heart of Bureaucracy

"Change everything as fast as you can (which is always faster than you think you can)." One of the traits of highly productive enterprises is that when they decide to do something, they do it swiftly and decisively. People who lead extremely efficient organizations agree that slow, ponderous change leaves everyone paralyzed with fear for weeks or months. Waiting for the other shoe to drop is far more painful than moving quickly to achieve the desired result. Any manager who believes an organization will fix itself over time is delusional.

"Get the right people on the bus." A leader or manager must rapidly ascertain who believes in, supports and will enthusiastically champion the chosen destination. Those people who work against the goal must be dismissed. Managers must come to realize a brutal truth: anyone not proactively supporting a chosen direction will consciously or unconsciously work to subvert it.

"Blow up functional silos and construct crossfunctional teams." As long as individual departments stand alone like impenetrable silos on the Kansas prairie, the primary efforts of the people inside them will be about defending their fortress from attack. The company must change the minds of people who protect their individual silo/empires and where that attempt fails, replace them with people who will focus on building more productive business units.

"Decentralize to create entrepreneurship." Zollars describes this as getting decisions closer to the customer and out of the "Palace of

Miracles"—the head office. As an example, in 1998 Yellow introduced a new service called Exact Express that promised to deliver a shipment within a one-hour window. The magic of the offer was that if the customer was unhappy for any reason about the service—even something as frivolous as not liking the driver's appearance—they could decide not to pay for it.

The product turned out to be a remarkable success in spite of the in-house grousing. Some of the remaining bureaucrats predicted that the company would go bankrupt because everyone would complain in order to get the service free. No way. According to Zollars, the amount the company writes off is infinitesimal by comparison to the additional millions in revenues linked straight back to the Exact Express initiative.

By moving the decision to the level of the customer instead of having a department of paper pushers haggling with clients, another part of the bureaucracy was eliminated.

"Flatten the organization to increase responsiveness to customers and others within the company." One powerful way to check on whether an organization is too fat is by running this simple test: When calling someone in the business—whether a department head, manager, owner or CEO—note whether your efforts are hindered by countless levels of gatekeepers. If so, chances are good you've stumbled onto a company that wants to prevent contact with the bosses. And if the boss is in hiding, so are countless others. Yellow tackled this problem by flattening the organization from eight layers to five.

When the boss responds immediately to customers and fellow workers, the stage has been set for productivity. The accessibility of the heads of highly productive businesses—like Dan DiMicco, who answers his own phone; Michael O'Leary, who sends his own faxes; and Bill Zollars, who answers his own e-mail—sends a resounding message throughout the organization that the days of bureaucracy are over.

"Create passion in the ranks: lead by visible example, show the troops you care—a lot!" The passion of a leader is demonstrated by Michael O'Leary's collecting boarding coupons and unloading luggage, Bill Zollars's nonstop year of travel to spread the message and Chairman Pat Lancaster's personally flying out to fix a customer's problem. It tempts credulity to ask any employee to be devoted to the objective of making the enterprise productive if their executives are not actively leading the way. Employees must be able to witness the passion of their leaders.

"Create and reinforce a high-performance culture." Among American workers, a frequently used response to the question "How are you?" is the downtrodden "Same s—, different day." That simply isn't the answer you'll receive in the highly charged environments of Nucor, SRC, Lantech, The Warehouse and Ryanair. The leaders of those companies know it's their singular responsibility to use every tool at their disposal, and to invent new ones if need be, to maintain an electric atmosphere. Zollars's formula: Use recognition, promotions and *greed*.

"View all decisions from the perspective of 'Does it help the customer?' and 'Does it make us money?' If it doesn't, it's bureaucracy. Shoot it!" We discovered the same mind-set at all productive companies committed to flattening the hierarchical structure. They've institutionalized the use of these two questions and ask them before making any decision.

Are Bureaucracies a Case of "Mine Is Bigger Than Yours"?

The contrast between the plush surroundings and multilayered bureaucracies of run-of-the-mill firms and what we found at the companies we studied is so dramatic that it raises a final question on the subject.

Why would any manager, owner or CEO spend money on opulent surroundings, corporate headquarters or showy perks, and why build or put up with ponderous reporting structures? This book is not the first place a manager, owner or CEO has read that bureaucracies make organizations less productive.

There are a few possible answers, but because psychological profiling (that's your clue) isn't within the scope of my professional abilities, I'll refrain and limit myself to a single pair of questions. "Do these guys have a deep-seated need to have a bigger one (I'm talking about buildings and bureaucracy, of course) than the other guys'?" And "Do women managers and executives have the same need?"

Highly productive companies prove the proposition that *Less Is More* by relentlessly striving to have no bureaucracy so that all their resources are directed at making more, serving more and selling more.

Once someone is committed to the task of destroying the bureaucracy, it's time to follow the lead of other highly productive companies and make a big statement to the entire organization about the new commitment to productivity.

And though nobody approves of public hangings, they do get the message across!

5

Get Rid of the Wrong Executives and Managers . . . Fast

If you are not fired with enthusiasm,
you will be fired with enthusiasm.
—Vince Lombardi

"What do you think this company needs more than anything else?" was the first question the board of directors of Yellow Corp. threw at new CEO Bill Zollars.

"Public hangings!" said Zollars.

Recalling the moment, Zollars now says he perceived panic and a collective gasp. Everybody in the room seemed to be wondering, "Oh, my God, what have we done bringing this guy here?"

"Public hangings?"

"Yep, public hangings!"

Bill Zollars had moved from Ryder Truck in Florida to Overland Park, Kansas, hoping to reverse the fortunes of the firm, determined to turn it into an enormously successful and productive company. But soon after his arrival, having scoped things out, he realized that dramatic action would be required to accomplish this goal. Yellow, a once-great freight company, was in serious trouble.

A Company That Had Lost Its Way

As members of a society long used to getting what we want, when we want it, most people take for granted that everything magically ends up where it's supposed to be, with little thought given to how it got there. Everything we eat, work with and touch in the course of our daily lives was *freight* at one time. And almost all freight travels by truck. (Eighty percent of all freight in the United States moves by truck, with the remaining twenty percent shared equally by air, boat and rail.)

Yellow began in 1915 when Cleve Harrell launched a taxicab service in Oklahoma City to haul soldiers from the railroad station and the outlying army base. In an effort to differentiate himself from all the other black taxis he painted his single cab bright yellow. Derided by the competition as the "banana taxi" his one car quickly became three and legend has it that John Hertz, the founder of Yellow Cab and Hertz, got his idea for painting his taxis yellow from Cleve Harrell.

Wanting to expand his fledgling taxicab company, Harrell asked his older brother to invest in the business. A.J. had been the first family member to settle in Oklahoma when, after visiting the 1904 World's Fair in Saint Louis, he'd decided to seek his fortune out west. He never got further than Oklahoma City, at the time a rough and tough town gushing oil and opportunity.

Described by former company historian Kent Politsch as "the most tightfisted man who ever lived," A.J. claimed he could make money doing anything. Already well off from ventures in horse trading, mule-drawn wagons, oil drilling and cattle ranching, he and his brother entered into a fifty-fifty partnership and formed Yellow Cab and Transit Company.

The brothers agreed that Cleve would run the taxi and operations while A.J. would concentrate on the trucking of freight. Everything went well until the brothers had an argument. Lips were sealed and no one ever said what the fight was about (though speculation centered on a woman), but the brothers split the business in two: Cleve took the taxi business and astute A. J. the trucking line. The brothers never spoke again. Whatever their argument was about it was so bad that years later, when Cleve died, the brothers still hadn't talked and A. J. paid his respects to his brother's family by driving by the church, rolling his window halfway down and offering his condolences.

There were no large, established freight companies; trucks were a new invention and there were few roads to drive them on. Freight companies were essentially mom and pop businesses that sprouted up in towns and cities across the nation.

By the mid-1940s, A. J. Harrell had grown the company to $3 million in annual revenues and six hundred employees. In his early sixties, in failing health and having grown weary of running the business, he sold the company to Arlington W. Porter, a New York investor, who proceeded to simultaneously expand, acquire smaller hard-pressed rivals and loot the company while engaging in practices that would make some of the evil, high-flying CEO bandits of the late 1990s and early 2000s proud.

In an early move he transferred ownership of all the company trucks (which under Harrell had always been paid for in cash) to a subsidiary and mortgaged them to the hilt. Rather than own its trucks the company now leased them. The official Yellow balance sheet didn't reflect the debt and rather than use the proceeds to grow the business he personally pocketed hundreds of thousands of dollars. His antics were probably sufficient to cause the company's immediate failure, but he was able to continue playing the game for a few years because of excitement about the enactment of the Federal Highway Act, under which all U.S. cities with more than fifty thousand residents would be connected by highways. The buzz was that the new interstate highway program would be a huge boon for trucking companies.

In 1948 Porter died unexpectedly and his widow turned the company over to a handful of cronies who through bad decisions, sloppy record keeping and grandiose plans managed to force the company to seek bankruptcy protection by 1952. Porter's widow, who'd expected a windfall, got nothing and the company owed vendors and the government millions of dollars and was placed in the hands of trustees.

George Powell, a Kansas City banker who had spent five years running a trucking company, learned of Yellow's problem and quickly gathered a group of investors and offered to loan Yellow $750,000 to pay off its debts in exchange for stock. The bankruptcy court accepted the offer and Powell and his son took over the company. The Powells immediately kicked out the previous management, got rid of the subsidiaries that had been used to hide Porter & Company's financial shenanigans, began maintaining the rolling stock, restored precise schedules and prioritized long-haul traffic. The group, who had ten months' worth of operating capital, eked out its first profit in four months.

For the next thirty years the Powell family led the company from one success to another, growing revenues from $7 million to more than $2 billion and eventually taking the company public. Without attempting to minimize the contributions of the Powells, it should be pointed out that once they'd cleaned up the mess they'd acquired and decided to focus exclusively on long-haul shipping and tapped the stock market for working capital, their job was a relatively easy one; freight rates were set by the Interstate Commerce Commission and as long as a company kept expenses lower than their revenues profitability was assured.

Trouble loomed large in 1980 when the U.S. government announced sweeping deregulation of the trucking industry. Yellow was headed for more than a decade of trouble. Lower-cost, nonunion rivals steadily chipped away at its revenues and the company, by then headed by grandson George Powell III, tried zigging and zagging and eventually engaged every alphabet-soup management theory in the book to reverse their steadily declining fortunes. None worked. In 1995, after several years of embarrassing losses, George Powell resigned and in 1996 the company recruited A. Maurice Myers as CEO. Myers had been instrumental in leading America West Airlines out of bankruptcy and earlier he'd steered Aloha Airlines out of serious trouble and into market leadership in the Hawaiian market with more than a 60 percent share. Within only months of his arrival, Myers was named chairman and a search was on for a CEO to take the reigns of a seriously troubled Yellow. That man was Bill Zollars.

Under Zollars's leadership, within only a few years Yellow achieved dramatic increases in all measures of productivity in the freight business including: dock bills per hour, tons per tractor per year, on-time service, decreased days in transit and customer satisfaction. Today Yellow is a $3.5 billion freight giant boasting roughly 50 percent more annual revenue than its rivals Consolidated Freight and Roadway.

Zollars contends that a new business owner, manager, department head or CEO committed to changing a business needs to send a loud message to everyone within the organization that things are going to change. His dramatic "public hangings" metaphor helps convey that message. "You've got to take the people who don't fit what you're trying to get done and move them out of the company fast."

Lee Iacocca had a sign posted behind his Chrysler office desk that warned, THE FLOGGINGS WILL CONTINUE UNTIL MORALE IMPROVES. The dynamic drama of these irreverent words told people to get with the program or get out. Like Iacocca, Zollars started with his attention-getting "public hangings" message and moved forward from there. There's nothing wishy-washy about this guy.

Basic truths must be confronted if a manager is serious about building a new culture of productivity. Increasing productivity is out of the question if even some of the executives and managers are clueless or bent on subverting the achievement of the owner's, manager's or CEO's BIG objective.

Dr. Linda Trevino swallowed hard when she first heard the phrase "public hangings." But Dr. Trevino, who is professor of ethics and chairwoman of the Department of Management and Organization at Smeal College, Pennsylvania State University, fundamentally agrees with Zollars. She says that when given a mandate to change an organization, there's a small window of opportunity to get rid of people who don't agree with the new direction or don't have the required skill sets. She maintains that a new executive has a honeymoon period of no more than six months to weed out people who need to be replaced and to assemble a new team of "A" players.

"When someone is determined to make the organization more productive, there are several questions they should ask themselves," she says.

"What do I have in mind for the future of the organization and what will my strategy be—those are the first questions. Then the manager must analyze the human capital and determine whether he or she has the right people to help formulate and implement the new direction." If not, Dr. Trevino believes, "It's the absolutely right thing to do to make changes and get rid of them.

"Everyone knows that it's harder to transform a culture than it is to U-turn a truck without brake fluid," she insists. "If you really want to make a difference, you have to send a strong signal that things are changing. One way to do that is to replace personnel at high levels. Obviously, the higher the level of person you're letting go, the more people will notice."

But she offers a cautionary note. "The manager contemplating significant personnel changes had better be ready with a big strategic initiative. And be prepared to truthfully explain to people what happened, and why, and who will be leading them or directing their efforts."

Bill Zollars moved decisively to fill the newly vacant positions with people who were committed to sharing his BIG objective. He then began his indefatigable year-long effort to get everyone onboard with his dream of transforming Yellow from a trucking company into a truly customer-focused transportation solutions company.

Yellow Corp., Ryanair, IKEA, The Warehouse, SRC, Lantech, World Savings and Nucor are productive companies that agree on a practice that says, "If you don't want to be a participating member of our culture, there's no place here for you." None of them is the least bit shy about offloading executives and managers who don't share and express a supportive zeal for the BIG objective.

Many Managers Are Too Chicken to Play Hangman

Because of a personal reluctance to dismiss the fellow executives and managers who are incapable of transforming their company into a productive powerhouse, many businesses get stuck in a quagmire of same old, same old. When quizzed as to why they tolerate incompetence among the executive ranks, most give a knowing nod and offer a response along the lines of, "You just can't fire people anymore. You'll get sued."

And so at many businesses it remains business as usual. *Unproductive* business as usual. Instead of terminating executives and managers who should be "hung," leaders turn their collective heads to watch business rivals become more productive. They see the competition whizzing by and wonder what magical solution eluded them.

A recent story, "Sometimes You Have to Fire People," published in the newsletter *Harvard Management Communication Letter* tells about a firing gone awry and maybe helps explain why many executives have become paralyzed when it comes to firing people.

"A sales manager at a national company," the author wrote, "was the subject of sexual harassment complaints in four different offices. To its credit, the company [conducted] a thorough investigation and found there was overwhelming evidence against him. The company president called him in to fire him. But the president was too embarrassed to discuss the real reason for the termination and blurted out: 'Bernie, we think it's time you retire.' The boss may have believed he was giving the manager a graceful way out of the company. He was wrong. 'Instead of doing the right thing for the principal reason, he found himself on the wrong end of an age discrimination complaint, which cost the company a lot of money to get out of,' says Jeff Pasek, a labor lawyer at Cozen and O'Connor in Philadelphia who dealt with the case."

By the time a story like that makes the rounds and is given differing spins by journalists, plaintiffs' attorneys and HR folks trying to bolster their own importance, many managers start believing the folklore that there's a flock of attorneys circling above them like vultures over roadkill ready to swoop down and sue them any time they fire someone. And that's not the reality.

In the story, the true culprit was a boss who was too much of a wimp to be honest, a leader who chose to play the easier role of good old boy (and we're talking sexual harassment here—duh!). That's why his company got taken to the cleaners. Consider the lost opportunity for a moment. He could have been seen as someone faithfully enforcing his company's stated code of conduct (the tom-tom drums beating constantly in every company ensure that eventually the word gets out) but because he didn't have the fortitude to hang someone, he ended up looking like an idiot. This spineless company chief was guilty not of discrimination but of wimping out in a difficult confrontational situation. The CEO knew what he meant to say, but when he opened his mouth, something else came out.

Dr. Trevino comments that the easy excuse when someone is afraid to be forthright is to say, they "can't do it" or that they "aren't allowed to do it." She adds, "Even my graduate students are surprised to learn that in the U.S. we go by the doctrine of at-will employment: unless someone is a member of a protected class (age, religion or race) and can actually prove discrimination because of class status, they don't have a valid argument. Courts actually have a small tolerance for unjustified discharge cases."

Most people would tell you that the worst thing they ever had to do in their working life was to fire someone. Because no one takes lightly the placing of a thick noose around a coworker's neck and pulling the lever, the deed too often goes undone or gets delegated away. As a sad result, team leaders, managers and some executives who are not helping build a more productive organization remain in their positions. So the foot draggers just go through the motions, using up oxygen, contributing nothing to company improvements.

Bill Zollars steeled himself for the job he had to do by reminding himself of several things. "First," he says, "you think about the people you're about to fire knowing it's not fair to them to keep them onboard because they'd be miserable going in the direction you're headed.

"The second thing you think about is the alternative and tell yourself that if you don't get them out of the place there might not *be* a 'place' and you'd all end up going down with the ship."

Zollars concludes, "Fear—the fear of knowing that nothing good will happen until these people are gone—is my best motivator for just getting it done."

Highly productive companies prove the proposition that *Less Is More* by quickly offloading and removing executives and managers who are incapable of helping the organization achieve their objectives.

While our research turned up a plethora of evidence testifying to the efficacy of public hangings as a way of sending out a big and clear message by sacking managers and executives who "don't get it," we found nothing to suggest that our organizations have any need for this tough tactic with workers.

On the contrary, all of the productive companies we studied for this book seem to value and respect their workers far more than the typical company. And as if to prove the point, each has created a culture that can best be described as egalitarian.

Though executives and managers who are guilty of not getting it, or who won't get it, are occasionally hung in public as a means for sending a loud message throughout the entire organization, this isn't a tactic that highly productive companies use with their workers.

In fact, as you're about to learn in the next chapter, just the opposite is true.

6

No Layoffs

In Japan, employees occasionally work themselves to death. It's called Karoshi. I don't want that to happen to anybody in my department. The trick is to take a break as soon as you see a bright light and hear dead relatives beckon.

—Scott Adams, *The Dilbert Principle*

A problem that vexes almost every business is head count.

Each person hired by an enterprise represents an increase in its fixed overhead costs of doing business. The problem of course is that revenues aren't fixed; they are every business's GIANT variable. So, when sales fall for whatever reason (recession, competition, local market conditions, drought, terrorist acts, overly exuberant *cough-cough* sales forecasting—pick your excuse) managers often believe their only recourse is to lay people off.

We were only able to document one bona fide layoff (a small one at Lantech that Chairman Pat Lancaster says occurred only after every other available option was exercised and everyone was rehired within a few months) at our productive companies. Considering that they represent a very broad range of business activities, from heavy manufacturing to retail, light manufacturing to transportation and financial services, and collectively employ more than one hundred thousand people, we think these companies have come closer to cracking the code on head count than other businesses.

One trait shared by all these productive companies is that they are essentially businesses with a simple business proposition working tirelessly to whittle away the unnecessary costs and edges, constantly becoming better and more efficient. And in the process each has created a workforce that doesn't spin its wheels on unnecessary projects, nonstrategic initiatives or flavor-of-the-month management philosophies. And *none* of them uses layoffs as a way to manage head count.

It's not believable or authentic when a corporate chieftain or manager publicly proclaims the organization's workforce as its biggest asset and then hastily retreats behind the closed door of his office to pen the orders for a layoff that lops off tens, hundreds or thousands of jobs. Too many ordinary companies, desperate to hit the next quarter's numbers or downsize to please the bankers, take an example from their buddies in other companies and reduce head count. Casual layoffs, which may have the seemingly happy side effect of momentarily nudging up the stock price, are in fact absolutely counterproductive in the long term.

Layoffs create more problems than they solve. Frequently, the employees who remain end up more concerned with their personal financial well-being than the company's productivity and become preoccupied, wondering if they'll be next, which often results in valuable workers seeking a more stable environment elsewhere. Eventually, assuming revenues start to improve, the company finds itself facing the costs of recruiting and training to fill the same positions they blew off during the reduction. The big whammy of course is the inability of an owner, manager or CEO to build any kind of productive culture in a business known for balancing its books by cavalierly offing people.

Dr. Linda Trevino says about layoffs, "I think they've become a management fad and companies do them because they think they're expected to, as everyone else is doing them. It's almost as though if you aren't doing layoffs you are somehow not lean and mean."

In her view, "Any company which sweepingly lays off workers is unlikely to be productive and must be judged as poorly managed. Productive companies have always known that employees are, indeed, their most valuable asset." She adds, "I'd also argue that if a layoff is needed, it's because the company wasn't managed very well to begin with. If a company has been keeping and developing its good people, evaluating everyone as they go along and not keeping those who aren't performing well, they wouldn't have a need for layoffs."

The best companies, she believes, do whatever it takes to avoid general layoffs. When a firm lets its employees know that they're cutting work hours instead of firing anyone, "they're sending a message to the employees that they are valued and that management will try very hard to protect their jobs." If the employees have been working hard, she says, this kind of announcement "is an exchange relationship."

At Nucor, where a significant part of the company's BIG objective is the promise there will never be a layoff, Dan DiMicco explains how the company handles down markets and cyclical demand for the steel it produces. "In a bad economy, the first thing to go is every executive perk and bonus," he says, "followed by plant managers and supervisors giving up theirs. Only then are the steel workers affected and we start by reducing a work week from five days to four and if that's not sufficient we might even go to three days even if we use one of those days cleaning the plant and doing housekeeping."

SRC's CEO Jack Stack also weighs in against layoffs. "Look," he says, "we have a tremendous passion for keeping and maintaining jobs. And so we've put our money where our mouth is." Employees are paid in four ways, he explains. In addition to salary, "we have a stock program where everyone earns stock based on the performance of the company. Then we have individual bonus programs tied to productivity and specific things we're trying to accomplish. Next, you've got the earnings of the company itself."

All of these come into play in a business downturn. "What we've built is a four-layer process to protect everyone here during tough economic times. The stock program would be affected before we'd ever cut a job. Next the bonus program would be hit and then a depletion of corporate earnings. These are the things we'd do before ever considering laying someone off.

"There have been times," says Stack, "when markets have collapsed and we've been devastated and we didn't lay anyone off. Sometimes it takes a long time to recover from those hits but you won't ever recover from them and move forward without your most important asset—good people."

Stack maintains that a business with a commitment to no layoffs must make certain in their planning process that they have a sufficient number of sales-forecast contingencies that allow them to deal with whatever happens in the marketplace. "We have a fifteen percent mentality here. We try to grow both sales and earnings fifteen percent a year. But we always factor in contingencies and trapdoors in order not to lay people off."

Highly productive companies have realized the pitfalls that await a firm when it attempts to balance its books by resorting to layoffs as a tactical response. The CEOs interviewed cited four undesirable consequences of doing so.

■ Organizations lose valuable knowledge when institutional memory is not transferred to others.

When employees leave, especially as the result of a layoff, the departing employees may not pass along the institutional memory they hold. Daniel W. Rasmus, vice president of Giga Information Group, has written, "As a knowledge management practitioner, when I look at layoffs, I see executives taking the easy way to cut costs—or give the impression that they're doing so—with little regard for the impact of workforce reductions on the long-term viability of the organization, let alone its people. And savings may not result. After all, it takes several thousand dollars to coach an employee to thrive in a position, and that investment is lost when the employee leaves. Then there is the issue of losing members who are vital in terms of their knowledge about their work and their connections to content, processes, and people. Surely there is a cost in this loss." (From "The Costs of Layoffs," *Knowledge Management*, June 1, 2001.)

▪ The damage to workers includes loss of morale, anxiety, pessimism and a "save-my-own-butt" attitude—a siege mentality that isn't in the best interests of the company.

Dr. Trevino points out that there's plenty of evidence backing this up. "We know that everyone within an organization pays close attention to a layoff because they know it's often not a single occurrence. Layoffs happen in stages. Instead of working, employees look for clues as to when it might happen to them and discuss among themselves how they'll be treated."

▪ It's more expensive to lay off workers (legal, administrative and financial packages out the door) and then rehire (recruiting and training expenses) than it is to shorten the workweek and temporarily reduce pay.

Journalist Victor Infante, who has extensively covered layoffs, sums up a secret that productive companies know. "Companies downsize to cut costs, but then are quickly forced to bring new people in because surviving employees leave for what they perceive to be more stable environments. This turnover starves production and lowers work quality." And he adds a thought that represents another way of looking at the cost issue: "Since the cost of a single new hire is generally equivalent to one year's salary, any savings from layoffs are negated."

Dr. Trevino agrees. "Although layoffs have been touted as good management, they actually do not have a positive impact on the bottom line."

▪ While layoffs may lead to superficial short-term efficiencies, they don't produce or sustain productivity.

Consultant Darrell Rigby has written, "[Companies] understand that although employee layoffs will reduce costs in the short term, the combination of severance expenses, loss of knowledge and trust, and subsequent hiring, training, and retention costs can quickly overwhelm expected savings." (From "Moving Upward in a Downturn," *Harvard Business Review,* June 2001.)

The Secret: Productive Companies Don't "Hire" Employees

In many businesses, the number of employees is merely a response to current market demand. If the market is hot for a company's widgets and they're having difficulty manufacturing and shipping enough of them, many firms simply hire some bodies and add another shift. A condition of employment frequently used by clueless companies when they're having a tough time finding people is, "Give them the mirror test. If they pass, hire them!" (Before the advent of modern science, the mirror test was a diagnostic tool to determine if someone was dead. As the story goes, a mirror would be placed above the mouth and nostrils of the body. If it fogged up from the person's breath, it proved they were still alive.)

As our research peeled away the glossy coverings of the world's most productive companies, what we found especially memorable was that, in addition to being immensely productive and profitable, each of these organizations is framed around a culture tenaciously

based on the true values of their workers. The infrastructure of productive enterprises includes a memorialized or unspoken but well-
understood promise: "We don't lay people off."

But just as highly productive companies don't lay people off, they
don't hire people until they get to know them. Since the employee
will often be with the company for the remainder of his or her
working career, the company is very careful about granting "membership."

Nucor's Dan DiMicco is ardent on the subject: "You have to hire
the right people. So the hiring process is a very important part of our
culture and our system. We've gotten better at applying tools to help
us pick the right people. And it's a very involved process.

"First we go through an extensive screening process filled with criteria we've developed over the years. Then we do interviews fitting
people to a psychological profile—even at the entry-level positions,
not just management. What we end up with are people who fit and
who will respond enthusiastically to our system. We take the time to
make sure that we hire accurately. Does that mean everybody we hire
makes it? No way. But very early on people find out for themselves.
And we find out if they're cut out to be a Nucor employee and can
grow to fit our culture."

The Warehouse's Stephen Tindall agrees; his company also employs extensive screening and interviewing to make certain they attract and hire the best people. In Tindall's view, the single most
important criterion is attitude. "When we're interviewing appli-
cants," he says, "it's much more about, 'Do these people fit with this
culture?' 'Are they the sort of people that subscribe to our values and
fit our company?'"

Ditto for all other productive companies. In every case we found
that the chief executive strongly believes that the people around him,
the people who report to him, the people at every level, represent the

company's biggest competitive advantage. So the people hired are extended invitations to membership even more carefully than a Park Avenue co-op selects its tenants. These singular enterprise leaders fight fiercely to protect the culture they've created. In return they receive unparalleled productivity from their people.

Because members of the human species fight to protect what they consider valuable, it wasn't surprising to learn that each of the productive companies we studied treats the hiring of people more like extending *membership* in an exclusive club than offering someone a job.

Once membership in a very special organization has been offered and after a mutual decision has been made, you can expect that the new employee will fight fiercely for the well-being and success of the organization—including doing things that might not be part of an original job description.

As a demonstration of just how strongly people desire membership in a special club and want to work for companies that value people, when Nucor announces the construction of a new plant and the intention to hire six hundred new workers, it is besieged by as many as six thousand people showing up to apply for jobs even though their salaries (remember this week's paycheck is for how much steel you produced last week) are far below other steel manufacturers' and the plants are located in small, out of the way rural locations.

While we were interviewing Stephen Tindall of The Warehouse he was interrupted by scores of people who had been bused in for a "demonstration." (There's a word that'll scare a business owner or manager.) It seems that more than 80 percent of the citizens of a New Zealand town had signed petitions (*ugh*—another scary word) asking the company to build a store in their town. Not only people but entire communities want to be part of a special club.

The Term "Head Count" Raises a Big Question

In the process of questioning the people who lead and manage some of the most efficient and productive businesses in the world, eventually I'd bring up the issue of "head count" management. Everyone seemed to bristle when the subject was raised. Not so much at the question as at the term itself.

Use of the current buzz phrase "head-count management" says a lot about the person or company using the phrase. It reveals the smug superiority of the those employing the words: *they* are the ones doing the counting. The expression gives away their view of the value of people: workers are only heads to be counted, added, subtracted and replaced at will. Finally, use of the phrase probably makes it easier to lay people off when the user isn't getting rid of Charlie, Jane and Harry but just a bunch of heads.

In recent years, as all enterprises have come under pressure to improve productivity, collectively they've employed a laundry list as long as your arm of tactics to deal with head count. A few of the more popular are outsourcing, contracted workforces, flextime workers, job sharing, multiple skilled workers, work-at-home programs and so on. Scores of books have been written touting the value of each.

While the companies we researched utilize many of the same options for managing the number of people they employ, we uncovered a major difference between them and other businesses.

Many companies, in the interest of short-term growth and ambition, allow their business proposition to become unnecessarily complicated. In the process they end up employing too many people and find themselves constantly exasperated trying to steer a many-headed hydra. The moment something goes wrong, and an overly ambitious sales forecast is missed or the economy experiences a hiccup, they're left with no alternative but to reduce head count. Instead of addressing the fundamental question, "How in the hell did we lose our way?" they grab for an easy solution: layoffs.

Because highly productive companies have ruthlessly maintained simple and uncomplicated business propositions, they have been able to systematize every aspect of their business and have determined the essential elements that require their control, ownership and close supervision, and those that don't.

For example: During one head-count reduction exercise or another virtually all major mortgage-granting financial institutions got rid of their own staffs of appraisers and outsourced the process years ago. By contrast the system used at one S&L, World Savings, is built on having very few nonperforming loans or foreclosures on the books and the company employs its own staff of appraisers. Most banks are interested in getting an appraisal that justifies doing the deal. World is interested in an accurate appraisal to minimize its potential exposure. It's probably not coincidence that World's nonperforming loans are the lowest in the industry.

We've all heard the phrase "the devil is in the details," but most companies don't have time for careful scrutiny of every detail because they're chasing and being chased in too many directions.

Here are a few tactics highly productive companies successfully use to constantly become more efficient and productive in the practice of their simple business proposition.

Outsourcing

Efficient enterprises all constantly seek ways to outsource nonvital areas of the business that have become commoditized and offer no competitive advantage.

A good example of properly executed outsourcing is a decision Yellow Corp. made regarding its technology development. According to Jim Ritchie, CEO of Yellow subsidiary Meridian IQ, "We use an organization that bases most of its technology work in India. It provides us a follow-the-sun methodology whereby they perform the grunt work—basic programming—while we're asleep, and when we get up we do the checks and balances. It allows us to do technology work twenty-four hours a day. We've been able to do some remarkable things very, very quickly and, as an added benefit, from an expense standpoint it's been extremely cost-effective."

But while having your code written in tech-savvy Bangalore is probably a fine idea, when you call a major retailer to schedule an appointment for appliance maintenance and your call is answered by an operator (think direct customer contact here) in another country who has difficulty with basic English language skills and repeatedly stumbles and bumbles his way through on-screen prompts, making a nightmare of the entire customer service process, then outsourcing hasn't fulfilled its intent.

While many companies have moved to the wholesale outsourcing of everything that isn't nailed down, there's a flip side of the coin. Studies, including one conducted by Ernst & Young, demonstrate that as many as 36 percent of respondents were unhappy with the quality of service provided by outsourced services. A further 28 percent claimed that outsourcing had taken up additional management time and only 18 percent said it had reduced costs.

Productive companies only outsource those functions that have become commoditized and refuse to outsource anything that might potentially offer them a competitive advantage.

Technology

One way to reduce the need for lots of people is to use simple technologies in ways that aren't obvious. In the next chapter you'll meet Herb and Marion Sandler, the co-CEOs of World Savings, a husband and wife team who have built from scratch the nation's most productive savings and loan. But as a sneak preview of the efficiency with which their company is run, this is what you'd hear if you called World wanting to sell them something:

Thank you for calling World Savings. Please listen to this message. Due to the high volume of calls received from outside vendors calling to solicit their products and services, we must ask that you forward in writing a description of your product or service along with any other information on your organization to World Savings and Loan, 1901 Harrison Street, Oakland, California 94612. Attention: Information Systems Department. You can be assured your information will be forwarded to the appropriate staff for review. If they find your company of interest to our business they will contact you directly at a later date. Thank you for calling World Savings. Good-bye.

Consider the implications of that message and the hundreds of thousands of people hours it saves each year. The message firmly states that the caller isn't getting through to a person and provides no option for doing so. If you've ever worked with salespeople, you know that most would simply give up and move on. The message directs callers to submit whatever they're selling in writing—which some number north of 90 percent will never do, opting to look elsewhere for easier prey. It succinctly states that the company does things on its own timetable and in its own way. And like everything else about the Sandlers and the company they lead, it's polite. For those salespeople who do bother to send material, the submissions aid World's negotiating hand for comparison shopping when they find something they're interested in.

While we were unable to locate any studies that indicate how many hours the average employee or manager spends dealing with telephone calls and meetings with vendors, suppliers and salespeople, based on personal experience we'd suggest it's close to 20 percent. Imagine using a simple piece of telephone technology to immediately improve your productivity 20 percent or render 20 percent of the staff redundant.

Consider the number of people it would take for a company like World Savings, which spends hundreds of millions of dollars annually on personnel, supplies and services, to deal with the thousands of salespeople who would like to sell it something.

Was this tactic for dramatically reducing the number of people required to deal with vendor and supplier calls and meetings just a brainstorm someone at the company had one day? Not! Because they never allowed themselves to take their business in dozens of different directions or adopt what Herb Sandler calls "the ready, fire, aim" mentality of most businesses, they have lots of time to constantly ask the question "What inefficiencies do we still have in our system that we can get rid of?"

I suspect that when many people read about the preceding tactic a light will go off and effective tomorrow they'll have their phone systems using a copy of the World Savings telephone message. To only use the message tactically would be to miss the entire point. Productivity and efficiency isn't the implementation of a collection of cute tactics but instead a nonstop journey whose destination is the elimination of all wasted time and effort.

Cross-training

When the workers in a business are cross-trained a company can often avoid layoffs through the use of attrition. Cross-training delivers another palpable advantage as well: a company with versatile employees and executives requires fewer layers of bureaucracy because everyone knows the nuts and bolts of the place.

Cheryl Billington of Yellow Corp. says, "When we dismantled the

bureaucracy and began bringing people out of their silos and assign-
ing them to projects different than those they'd ever worked on before, we reaped other benefits as well. Now, I might say, 'Hey, you
know a lot about sales and marketing systems but I'm going to have
you work in operations for a while.' The net result is that we're able
to leverage our investment in people and use that knowledge to
come up with better solutions for our customers."

Work at Home

Many of the companies we studied employ workers whose offices
are based at home.

Consultant Jack Nilles of JALA International is the man who
coined the word "telecommuter." According to him, in year 2002
more than twenty-one million people were working at home and the
number is growing by 15 percent to 20 percent each year. Nilles says
there are three distinct benefits that a company can gain by allowing
members of the workforce to function from their homes.

"The first thing that occurs if telecommuting is done properly," he
says, "is that productivity immediately increases on average by ten to
twenty percent."

In addition, says Nilles, "the savings in facility costs can be tremendous. IBM alone has saved more than one hundred million dollars in
lower rents, parking and infrastructure from having a telecommuting
workforce."

The biggest benefit of a work-at-home team, according to Nilles,
is that it tends to be more loyal. "Who'd want to leave a job where
you get to work out of your home, be paid on a performance-based
system and not have some bureaucrat constantly nosing over your
shoulder?"

However, Nilles cautions that unless a stay-at-home workforce is
properly set up, a company can find a fiasco on their hands. "Workers first have to be taught to work from home and managers have to

learn to manage a team they can't see." It's vital, he insists, that time be closely counted, people kept accountable and compensation be performance-based for best results.

According to one study reported in the *Harvard Management Communication Letter* in May 1999, "82.6% of telecommuters reported increase in productivity since beginning to work at home while 100% of their managers agreed their workers had either become more productive or sustained their productivity."

One-Time Reorganization Layoffs

Occasionally, a new manager, owner or CEO will decide that a significant reorganization (and an attendant layoff) is required to make the business unit more productive. Prior to the layoff, it's the responsibility of the leader to determine where the organization is going (the simple BIG objective again), and determine who on the executive team they'll count as their ranking officers. Only then will the leader be ready to commence a one-time layoff, accompanied by an honest explanation and assurances that layoffs will not become the company's way of life.

Any manager or executive who violates the one-time rule should be told the story about the three envelopes. Here it is, once again, to refresh your memory and to give fair warning:

The first day on the job as a new manager, an executive found three sealed envelopes numbered 1, 2 and 3, along with a note from his predecessor. The cover note told the new manager to open a letter each time he faced a major problem.

Within a few weeks a huge problem arose and the manager opened up the first letter. It said, "Blame it on me!" The executive did that and the situation settled down quickly. But within a few months another crisis raised its ugly head and the manager opened the second letter. "Announce a major reorganization," it said. Which the new executive promptly did, and again things quieted down. When the next big problem confronted the manager, he opened letter number three. It simply said, "Write three letters."

Most people in the workforce are able to understand the need for a one-time major reorganization. But nobody worth their salt wants to work in an unenlightened environment where each time the top dog confronts a problem, the only response offered is "Let's reduce head count."

Highly productive companies prove the proposition that *Less Is More* by hiring carefully and having a policy of no layoffs, which creates a workforce that feels safe and secure and committed to achieving the goals and ambitions of the enterprise.

Another observation from our research is that highly productive companies, by comparison to their less efficient competitors, don't seem to make many bad decisions that end up distracting them and causing them to lose their productive edge. The pieces of the decision-making puzzle finally came together when we went deep inside America's most productive financial institution. That's where we're headed next.

7

WTGBRFDT?

A wise man makes his own decisions;
an ignorant man follows the public opinion.
—Chinese proverb

In our study of productive companies, we uncovered a single question that the people routinely ask before making any business decision. It's a powerful question that every business seeking increased productivity should instill so thoroughly that everyone repeats it like a mantra before every decision.

Though we encountered the question being routinely asked at all productive companies, one standout among them has become huge and successful largely through the institutionalization of this single, simple question. That one company is World Savings.

A Husband and Wife Team = A Model of Productivity

"How do you manage to run such a huge financial institution and spend so little money doing it?" is my first question for Marion and Herb Sandler, the husband-and-wife team who run publicly traded Golden West Financial (GDW), the parent of World Savings. Hearing the question, they look at each other and share a knowing glance. Herb Sandler answers first.

"I'm not sure," he says, looking at me solemnly. "That's a very good question."

Uh-oh, I think. I've fought hard for their cooperation and wonder if I've blown it by asking a very direct question too early on.

"Instead of asking us how we manage to spend so little"—and here Herb pauses and then breaks into a broad grin—"maybe you should ask our competitors how they're able to spend so much."

"Look," Marion joins in, leaning closer to the conference table and speaking softly but firmly to make her point, "we would honestly like to know how our competitors are able to spend as much as they do running their businesses. We simply don't understand how they do it."

Marion and Herb Sandler have spent most of their married life, the past forty years, working together every day and questioning why other financial institutions do things the way they do. In the process of answering their own questions, they've built one of America's biggest financial powerhouses.

With 462 offices in thirty-eight states, World Savings in 2001 originated $21 billion in mortgages and served more than one million customers whose deposits totaled a record $35 billion. The Sandlers and a close-knit group of company insiders own 20 percent of the company's shares, a holding that in early 2002 was worth $2 billion. For thirty-five years, without missing a beat, the company has achieved 20 percent average annual compound growth each year.

Its success is even more dramatic when compared with the rest of the industry. In the 1980s, a combination of deregulation, a bad economy and bad loans by the bushel sent the U.S. savings and loan industry into a tailspin. More than half of the 4,500 S&Ls in the nation shut their doors, got sopped up or were forced out of business by the feds after the government began stepping in to ensure the industry's solvency. The Sandlers were invited to Washington to help the senior staff of the Securities and Exchange Commission understand what had happened. One of the documents at that 1980s meeting listed the nation's top twenty thrifts. Today, World Savings is the only one that remains from the list.

World Savings is a case study in productivity. The Sandlers run the company with little more than half the employees of their closest competitor. The average World Savings employee generates an astounding $752,000 in revenue each year. That is 40 percent more than the industry average. Each employee contributes $145,000 in profit annually, which represents nearly double the industry average.

The savings and loan business model is a fairly simple proposition. People deposit money with an S&L and are paid interest on their savings. The firm uses those deposits to fund mortgages, keeping the difference between what they pay in interest and what they receive. While almost everyone else managed to muck up a simple proposition, the Sandlers not only survived but created one of the most efficient and productive money machines on the planet.

The couple met in 1960 while walking on a beach in the Hamptons. Herb Sandler, a brash young attorney who grew up on New York's Lower East Side, tried to impress Marion Osher by rambling on about his knowledge of Wall Street (which he freely acknowledges was almost nonexistent). What he didn't know was that sharpminded and analytical Marion was one of only three women in nonclerical jobs on Wall Street and was already an accomplished stock market analyst with enough knowledge of the markets to skewer him if she wanted. Instead she married him.

Marion followed savings and loans for Oppenheimer, her employer, and the more she studied them the more she became convinced that the industry was undermanaged. Constantly reminded at Oppenheimer that she'd never be allowed to make partner because she was a woman, she decided not only would she manage something but that the something would be an S&L. She and Herb would do it better than anyone else. In for a penny, in for a pound, she reasoned.

Marion decided to solve her allergy problems at the same time. So within two years of being married, the new Sandler duo was ready to fulfill Marion's ambition; the young couple headed to the warm climes of California to buy a savings and loan.

After searching for six months they finally found Golden West Savings in Oakland, an industrial city just across a bridge from its more glamorous and famous neighbor, San Francisco. When they set their sights on Golden West in 1963, it had two small branches and $38 million in assets. The family who owned the company was willing to sell it for $3.1 million.

"I had zero money . . . *nada*," says Herb, holding up his hand and forming a zero with his thumb and index finger. "Marion had a small bit of money from an inheritance and some other family members were willing to help us with a down payment." Together the couple scraped together $600,000 and went to search for financing. They were turned down a number of times, including by Bank of America, which couldn't see why they should finance a potential rival.

But the deal got done. Herb and Marion went to work in the branches and immediately began asking questions, lots of them. After forty years of asking questions about their industry and analyzing every bit of information, they've become two of the most respected operators in the business. But their practices are frequently misunderstood. Analyst reports often are written to delight readers with anecdotes that magnify the tightfistedness of the Sandlers, an attitude toward thrift that has become a legend in its own time.

Yet in scores of interviews with executives, employees, vendors, suppliers and customers, we failed to turn up any evidence of their being cheap. Instead we learned that their thrift represented the Sandlers' deep-seated abhorrence of waste.

Spending time with the Sandlers can be mentally exhausting. They're both high energy and as soon as one comes close to finishing a thought (sometimes even before), a spouse rallies another well-aimed ball over the net.

In our sessions, they both took shots aimed at ideas and people considered pillars of the financial world. Herb and Marion were each eager to express their disrespect for doing things in ways they'd always been done, their disdain for the time-honored but nonproductive traditions of the corporate and financial communities. The Sandlers are proud to describe themselves as iconoclasts.

As you've already discovered from this book, each highly productive company we encountered has a clear and simple BIG objective. The World Savings BIG objective was quite obvious.

Marion Sandler had always known she wanted to run something. "I was always entrepreneurial and in every place I ever worked I'd figure out what they were doing that I wouldn't do and ask myself how I'd change it." Until World Savings, Marion had to tolerate the frustration of not being able to carry out her vision. "I could analyze the problem, see the opportunity and knew what needed to be done but never had the authority to execute."

That, and the added baggage on Wall Street of knowing she'd never become a partner. But another factor motivated them, as well, Herb explains. "We'd both experienced working for people who were significantly less able than we were. It's very frustrating to work for people who exercise authority and aren't particularly competent.

"For us," says Herb Sandler, "owning our own business meant freedom and not having to work in that type of environment. Our early work experiences had a profound impact in shaping our business." The Sandlers simple big objective was to build a business where reward and promotion would be based solely on merit, free from the injustices and unfairness they'd witnessed and experienced.

As the Sandlers speak about the principles they used to build their business, it is hard not to feel an almost eerie sense of déjà vu. Herb and Marion use words to describe their guiding principles that are nearly identical to words we had heard at Nucor, The Warehouse, SRC, Yellow Corp., IKEA, Ryanair and Lantech.

"The companies we'd worked for had been highly bureaucratic organizations where you couldn't get anything done," says Herb. "And they were all political. Our first promise was that we'd never be bureaucratic or political."

He tells the story of an acquisition to illustrate his argument. "We were in the process of acquiring another company, and during the time you're in contract to buy another firm, there's obviously a need for frequent communication.

"At one point," he says, "Marion called the person in charge of marketing with a question about something and I promptly got a call from the CEO telling me that's not the way things work. He told me that Marion should have called him and he would have relayed the request to the head of marketing, who'd talk to the proper supervisor in the marketing department, who would talk to the right employee, who would get back to the supervisor, who'd get back to the head of marketing, who'd relay the information to the CEO, who would then call me."

Herb Sandler's blunt observation: "That type of bureaucracy is common in many companies. We won't have that crap around here. It reminds me," he says, "of the old story about Merrill Lynch. You go into a Merrill Lynch office and ask, 'Who's in charge here?' and all fifteen hands go up in the air. Then you ask, 'Who's responsible?' and all fifteen hands come down."

"We also decided," says Marion, "that in building the organization, we would never allow it to be about us and our egos. We were determined to build a true meritocracy. At this company everybody takes responsibility and moves forward. Even when the company was privately held and we owned one hundred percent of the stock," she adds, "we gave stock options. Our philosophy has always been that those who participate in making the company successful should enjoy the fruits of that."

The early limitations placed on Marion because she was a woman provided the Sandlers with another guiding principle: the Sandler meritocracy would recognize women and the company would be inclusive in every way. "We were the first company with women loan representatives, loan salespeople, appraisers and branch managers," Herb proudly points out. "Other companies simply didn't do this back when we started our business. There were no women in any of those jobs. It's not rocket science to know that when you're hiring the best you're able to find from only fifty percent of the population, that you're disqualifying the other fifty percent. That's simply unfair and wrong."

Jumping into the fray, Marion is quick to add, "The other thing we didn't do was go out and hire figurehead branch managers. We simply didn't do it. We were committed, and are, to promoting from within and because most of the tellers were women, they became the universe from which we promoted."

Today the Sandlers' commitment to diversity is manifested on their company's board of directors. There are more women than men on the board, and Hispanics, Asians and African Americans are all represented. You get the feeling from the Sandlers that the makeup of their board has nothing to do with political correctness but instead embodies strict adherence to their stated principle: a true meritocracy.

Besides no politics and no bureaucracy, a meritocracy instead of an ego-driven culture, and a diverse workforce, the other principle Marion and Herb Sandler say they've always embraced is constant analysis of everything.

"When we were ready to begin expanding, one of the questions we asked was 'What's the purpose of a branch office?'" says Marion. "At the time, most financial institutions were building branches of ten thousand to fifteen thousand square feet, but a little industrial engineering makes you wonder why you need all that space. The purpose of a branch is to collect deposits from people. Why would you need fifteen thousand square feet to do that?"

"Our branches average about three thousand to four thousand square feet," says Herb. "Imagine how much more economically you can run a branch that's one-quarter the size of the other guy's."

Marion interjects, "It wasn't only the cost savings realized with a smaller branch but what was going on inside in these big vast spaces. There was always a male branch manager sitting on a pedestal whose job was to glad-hand people, while the real work was being done by a woman, the head teller/operations officer. We eliminated the position of male branch manager right away. They didn't do anything."

There's one example of the Sandlers' distaste for waste, told so many times by so many analysts that I suspect they copy one another's work. But having experienced this personally, the story bears repeating: When you visit the executive offices of World Savings in Oakland, you take a long elevator ride to an upper floor and upon disembarking walk into the reception area to find a vacant receptionist desk.

A sign on the desk directs you to call the person you've come to see and wait until they come to get you. By the sign is the telephone. ("I really wish people would stop calling it an old black telephone," says Marion. "It's not that old.")

She explains the arrangement by saying, "I can't imagine paying someone to sit out there all day doing nothing but smiling and greeting people."

But the Sandlers bristle at the slightest suggestion someone can build a highly productive enterprise by being cheap. "The art of being productive isn't whether you're saving costs," an animated Herb Sandler says, striding across the room. "It's how you spend money.

Spending money is an art. You spend money to be productive. You don't *not* spend money and become productive."

"That's a principle that pervades our entire organization," adds Marion. "We don't cut corners, we focus on productivity."

When deregulation set savings and loans free to do almost whatever they wanted, the Sandlers chose to steer World Savings down a simple and far more conservative course than their competition.

"All of a sudden," says Herb, "you could do all kinds of things you couldn't do before. You could make commercial loans, unsecured loans, offer discount brokerage services. Hell, even invest in windmill farms. All of a sudden it was ready, fire, aim for everyone else. That's not the way we do things. We're very analytical."

Here's the "Killer" Question

This brings us to the single big question promised at the start of the chapter. You can't be blamed if you wonder whether there really is a single question that businesses can use as a basis for every decision they're required to make. The answer is yes.

The question is simple but not simplistic.

I discovered that all the productive companies included in this book ask this one question each time they're required to make a decision. Unfortunately, the question is so straightforward that some readers will probably glide right over it and not give it the thought or consideration it deserves.

Setting us up for this, Herb introduces the topic by telling me, "Marion has a question that we ask all the time whenever we're required to make any decision." He warns that it's an astute question and therefore sometimes very complicated to answer, and then encourages her to share with me.

I edge up closer to the edge of my seat. I wonder, *Is this going to be the holy grail of business?*

Marion leans forward in her chair and speaks softly but firmly. "The question," she says, "the one we ask before we make any decision is, *'What's the good business reason for doing this?'*"

Now I suggest you pause to think about this question for a moment. *"What is the good business reason for doing this?"*

When you consider all the implications, the fundamental importance of the question becomes vividly clear. And yet, from your own experience in business, how often have you observed that question being thoughtfully considered before a manager, an owner or CEO makes any decision? Instead, decisions are most often based on the pressing needs and circumstances of the moment—in the popular phrase, "putting out fires." Imagine how many fewer people would be hired (who might eventually have to be laid off when the corporate coffers temporarily run low) if someone had paused to consider both the short- and long-term ramifications of a hiring by asking the fundamental question.

"When everyone else was rushing into all kinds of different loan products, we asked, 'What's the good business reason for doing this?' and couldn't come up with an answer," says Herb. When their competitors ran into big trouble as a result, Herb notes, "We didn't."

"The same thing happened with ATMs," adds Marion. "Every other institution was rushing to install ATMs and we kept asking the WTGBRFDT question and couldn't come up with the right answer." World eventually added ATMs only after deciding to offer a high-yield checking account likely to appeal to customers who would require the convenience of them.

"It was the same with free checking," Herb says, picking up the thread. "As soon as one institution began offering it, everyone else was jumping onboard. But the more we analyzed it and asked the question, 'What's the good business reason for doing this?' we couldn't figure it out. It seemed the only way to make it work for us was by screwing the customer and feeing them to death."

"Until we were able to find a niche, we refused to follow everyone else because there was no good business reason for doing it," states Marion.

When World found a niche and created a product that offered substantial interest rates for checking accounts with high balances, the money poured in. According to Herb Sandler, "It was like somebody opened the floodgates. While other banks were offering free checking and paying their customers between zero and one-half percent, and charging them fees for everything, we were paying five percent and the money cascaded in. Our productivity soared."

He poses the natural question and then answers it: "Because people who maintain large checking account balances tend not to write a lot of checks, they're very low-cost accounts to maintain. In the end everything worked for everybody. The customer got fantastic value. We got fantastic value. It was win, win, win!" he proclaims. "But only after we were able to figure out the good *business* reason for doing it."

I'd guess the Sandlers' often-repeated question can be infuriating at times. Even their agreeing to be included for study in this book didn't escape the challenge.

"Why were we willing to spend time with you?" Herb wonders aloud. "You're the first author we've ever agreed to meet with. Why? Are we doing it as a manifestation of ego?" he asks rhetorically. "No, it's because we asked ourselves the question, 'What's the good business reason for doing this?' and after checking you out, we decided that based on your previous work, you'd end up writing something that will accurately reflect the values of the company. The good business reason for doing it is that our employees will feel good about it."

Herb Sandler's description of a panel discussion sponsored by the Federal Home Loan Bank sums up why many businesses just can't get their productivity act together.

"Marion was scheduled to be on a panel; the subject was cost control and the talk before hers was on technology with John Fisher from Bank One. He was a real technology guru twenty years ahead of his time and the ballroom was packed with people hanging out the doors to hear him speak. As soon as he finished talking, half the people left and didn't stay for Marion's presentation on cost control. What's most ironic is that after she spoke a whole group of people came over to me. The gist of their remarks was 'I learned more from your wife in the last forty-five minutes than I've learned in the previous twenty years in business.' Fisher was talking bells and whistles and nobody did a damn thing as a result of his speech." Herb Sandler summarizes the experience by observing that most people would rather hear about what's new and exciting than hear about something that really works.

Today most of the World portfolio comprises loans on single-family homes up to four-unit buildings, though it does occasionally write multiple residential mortgages, and 95 percent of its mortgages are at adjustable rates—mortgages with interest rates that go up and down with the market. Imagine the potential plight of other institutions writing fixed thirty-year loans at low interest rates and later being forced by market conditions to pay more to attract deposits than they're earning on their loans.

Because the company requires substantially higher down payments on home loans than the rest of the banking industry, World assures itself of far fewer foreclosures and nonperforming loans than their competitors. The Sandlers believe the company policy is so vital to success they even employ their own appraisers, arguing that the fee-based appraisers used by most financial institutions will deliver the appraisal required to get the loan done and not necessarily deliver an appraisal that reflects a property's true worth.

World Savings attracts money from customers looking for competitive rates on their deposits. Most of its customers are mature people who are able to maintain significant checking and savings balances. Studies consistently demonstrate that older consumers are more reluctant to change for the sake of change. As long as World continues to offer high-yield saving devices, the customer base remains stable. Because of its low-cost, high-productivity structure, World is able to consistently offer a number of products with higher interest rates than other institutions.

World Savings is the quintessential example of a business that began with a simple BIG objective, whose leadership fought ruthlessly to maintain the simplicity of the proposition and that managed to systemize every aspect of the enterprise while simultaneously wringing out all excesses and inefficiencies.

By constantly asking a very simple question, "What's the good business reason for doing this?" the Sandlers have turned World Savings into a nearly bulletproof business model.

"Let's Just Do It" Doesn't Exist in Highly Productive Companies

Too many business decisions are made for wrong reasons.

Seemingly minor decisions are often hastily made just to get them done and off someone's desk, as though the ability to make snap decisions means someone is worthy of his or her sergeant stripes. "Go ahead and hire them if you need them, just get it done," commands one harried manager anxious to move on to something else that's been on his mind for a week or more. "Look, someone else is going to do it if we don't, so let's go for it," barks another. "We need to do *something*," says the buddy of a salesman peddling his wares. "Let's buy it."

Few people pause to answer the Sandlers' killer question, "What's the good *business* reason for doing this?" when making seemingly minor decisions.

And in most instances even major decisions do not undergo a litmus test about whether or not there's a clear and strong business reason for embarking on a particular course of action.

Some companies rush to market just to keep up with the competition. Others, in their haste to be first, introduce or release products or services before all the financial ramifications have been considered. Sometimes decisions are made for price cuts to capture market share and then, when copied by the lemmings, the product turns into a commodity, leaving minuscule margins. In other cases, hurry-up-hurry-up computer-industry salespeople peddle multimillion-dollar IT systems priced to get the iron off the docks and the revenue booked, while the gullible companies that buy the sales spiel end up with systems quickly rendered obsolete.

All because the killer question wasn't asked: *WTGBRFDT?*

When people want to understand and emulate the successful and highly productive Nucor model, CEO Dan DiMicco stresses to them, "Our culture is based on a long-term focus. When you examine everything and make all your decisions based on asking if it's a good business reason for the long term instead of if it's good for the short term, the answers you get will be very different."

Jack Stack of SRC offers an addendum to the question. "The first thing you have to ask," he says, "is whether it's a good business decision. But then you need to go one step further. Even if it's a good business decision, you still need to examine all the possible contingencies and have some trapdoors ready to open if it doesn't work out as planned."

Setting Aside B.S. and "Self"

You'll recall that when Herb Sandler asked Marion to share her "secret" question with me, before she responded, he added, "It's an astute question and sometimes very complicated to answer."

Having had the opportunity of collectively spending many hundreds of hours with the people who lead and manage these highly efficient organizations, there's an observation that applies across the board—an observation that stands in stark contrast to what most people witness while moving about the upper echelons of business: there's simply no bullshit and bluster, no sense of self-importance, about any of these people.

The question "What's the good *business* reason for doing this?" is as hard-nosed and brutal as it comes. A pompous poop with more ambition than talent, schooled in advancing up the structure on the basis of a gleaming smile, a sparkling personality, a firm handshake and making as few decisions as possible along the way, wouldn't be able to exist in—much less create or lead—a culture where every decision has to pass the muster of the killer question. That takes brains and understanding business propositions.

Answering the question is as demanding as Herb Sandler warns. It means always having a good business reason for defending a project or initiative, or risk being shot down. In a productive company the homework must be done. As Herb Sandler points out, "There are very few questions that can't be quantified."

Long after this book has come and gone, an image that will linger in my mind is that of meeting the Sandlers for our first interview. Dressed in his trademark vested suit, fit and slim, Herb would occasionally stand, pace the room and gesture boldly to make a point, while petite, demure and always razor-sharp Marion sometimes leaned intensely forward to stress an assertion . . . but otherwise sat calmly, *knitting* throughout the entire meeting. I remember wondering if she multitasks by nature, so averse to wasted time that she has to be producing something. Or perhaps she just likes to knit. In any case, that meeting created a powerful and memorable image.

I couldn't help but picture being a manager with World Savings, being summoned to her office for a meeting and being quietly asked the question "Jason, what's the good business reason for doing what you're proposing?" with her sitting quietly knitting away while I stumbled over my best-shot defense. I bet everyone at World Savings always stands ready to answer the WTGBRFDT question. (Marion later insisted she would never knit during a private one-on-one session and it's simply something she does to occupy herself during group meetings.) Knowing Marion as I do now, people need have no fear of where those knitting needles or the scarf they're making might end up. But possibly they have read *A Tale of Two Cities* and remember Madame Defarge.

Being able to lead and manage an organization by constantly asking, "What's the good business reason for doing this?" means completely setting aside ego, overcoming the need to defend previous decisions and possessing the ability to let go of the policies of yesterday that are no longer smart and on target. Notwithstanding how this couple might enjoy the personal fortunes they've accumulated (and I wasn't interested in going there), in the work environment each is a model of humility and modesty and acts as a responsible guardian of their investors' money.

Doesn't It Take a Lot of Time to Ask the Killer Question Before Every Decision?

Any enterprise willing to institutionalize and train everyone to ask the killer question will spend dramatically less time fixing bad decisions and correcting wasteful initiatives. The organization is likely to end up saving so much money previously wasted that it will always have sufficient cash reserves to move quickly and opportunistically whenever its leaders spot a great prospect for growth.

Asking whether it would slow down a business to use this question routinely is dragging in a red herring. Anybody who raises this challenge is a person who can't imagine functioning in a highly analytical and accountable environment. Each leader of the organizations we studied said the same thing. "Working for us isn't for everyone. It takes a special kind of person to follow our system." (And "system" is a word you'll find as the subject of a later chapter.)

Efficient businesses prove the proposition that *Less Is More* by having institutionalized programs in place for making solid business decisions.

Next, we discovered that highly productive companies demystify the role of the bean counters, eliminate accounting jargon and make the numbers easy. That's the lesson of the following chapter.

8

The Real Financial Drivers

Question: Why did the accountants cross the road?
Answer: Because the client told them to.

"Accounting is the enemy of productivity!"

So proclaims highly respected management consultant Dr. Eliyahu Goldratt, who has been described by *Fortune* magazine as a "guru to industry" and by *Business Week* as a "genius." His book *The Goal,* a business cult classic, has sold more than two million copies.

Some of Goldratt's arguments were compelling, so we followed his lead. With my researchers in tow, I poked my nose around the accounting departments of the companies we were studying, trying to learn how they handle accounting and financial reporting differently than their less productive rivals. I was sure that my search for accounting theories shared by the chosen companies would turn up something new and off the radar screens—and it did.

What we discovered is that highly productive companies use the accounting department as it was originally intended; for the preparation and presentation of accurate and truthful financial statements testifying to the *past* performance of the company and as a resource capable of answering the financial "what-if" questions put forth by management in scenario planning. And . . . nothing more.

We concluded our research by delving into the role of the

accounting and financial reporting functions of the companies we studied. We found the following four conclusions to be significant.

- Financial statements—the end results of accounting are the *real* enemy of productivity.
- Financial statements don't portray the realities required to increase productivity.
- Financial statements mask an embarrassing secret that prevents companies from becoming more productive.
- Truly productive companies use "Drivers" without wiggle room to increase real productivity.

Financial Statements

A financial statement is comprised of two components.

The first element is the balance sheet. It lists the assets and liabilities of a company and has as its primary purpose to reflect the net worth of the enterprise. It's essentially a snapshot or statement of a company's financial condition at a specific point in time.

The second part is the profit and loss statement commonly referred to as a P&L. It changes every month, quarter or year depending on how frequently a company generates one. It lists revenues and expenses for the reporting period and is designed to show the profits earned by the firm during the reporting period. A P&L is like a movie whose scenes change frequently.

Jean Cunningham, the CFO of Lantech, remembers her first days at the company, walking around and asking how each person used the firm's monthly financial statement. "Each of them kind of looked down, shuffled the papers on their desk and wouldn't even admit they did nothing with it. Finally, each of them told me that they usually filed it." With her eyes rolled back and a look of utter exasperation on her face, she adds the capper: "What they really meant was 'the round file,' the garbage can, because they didn't do anything with the darn thing. They didn't understand it."

At its best a financial statement is a complex and *historical* document that says nothing about productivity. Neither balance sheet nor P&L makes representations about past productivity, future profitability or the truest financial condition of a company.

Financial Statements Don't Reflect Productivity

Imagine playing a game of golf with a football. While the idea is laughable, so is trying to use a financial statement for anything other than its intended purpose—a look backward at a company's past performance. But that's the dangerous game most companies play.

Nowhere in a financial statement will you find the number of employees. Without this number there's no way to determine production, revenues or operating profit per person. A financial statement doesn't list how many customers a company has or how much the average customer spends or how long he or she remains a customer, and in no place will you find how much business the company has in the pipeline.

A financial statement respecting the essential power of productivity would be about how quickly The Warehouse can move goods from a receiving depot to the stores and achieve sell through, about how many customers refinancing a mortgage remain with World Savings rather than changing financial institutions and about how many seats Michael O'Leary is able to fill on a new Ryanair route.

Many Financial Statements Distort Reality

For purposes of tax reporting, financial statements are required by law to be generated in accordance with GAAP (generally accepted accounting practices). There are thousands of these principles that fill nearly 1,200 pages in the book *GAAP—Handbook of Policies and Procedures* and many more thousands of ways to interpret them. As you might guess, in an effort to make their financial statements as attractive as possible, businesses routinely resort to a Polonius kind of wisdom that says, "If you can't dazzle them with your brilliance, baffle them with your B.S." Accountants aggressively interpret each of these many principles to their advantage.

In January 2002, we learned from David Cay Johnston of the *New York Times* that Enron and its auditors, Arthur Andersen, had created and used almost nine hundred off-shore subsidiaries making sham transactions to minimize income taxes, thus setting itself up for almost $400 million in tax refunds while hiding billions of dollars in liabilities in off-balance-sheet subsidiaries.

Only months later, troubled Xerox reached a settlement with the U.S. Securities and Exchange Commission, which had filed a lawsuit against the company accusing it of fraudulently using its accounting to "burnish and distort" financial results for years. At the same time the SEC informed Xerox employees and former Xerox auditor KPMG that they might face charges of accounting fraud.

By the spring of 2002, General Electric was announcing massive layoffs from GE Capital, its financial services arm, as analysts like Robert Olstein of the Olstein Financial Alert Fund charged that GE's profit was based on "financial reengineering."

In an effort to show how productive it was at gaining new customers, publicly traded Adelphia Cable monetized as many as 600,000 nonexistent customers and let it hit the balance sheet, while DirecTV, a subsidiary of Hughes Electronics, did the same when it admitted counting as paying customers more than 360,000 people who had simply filled out credit applications.

Financial markets tumbled on the revelation that MCI WorldCom had failed to deduct nearly $4 billion from its revenues—counting them instead as capitalized expenses—resulting in tremendous losses rather than profits. Shares in the company, once valued at more than sixty dollars apiece, were quickly worth pennies.

And by the summer of 2002 everyone who follows business had learned a new accounting trick—"the round trip." My company and yours exchange $10 million worth of inventory on the same day. While no company is better off for the transaction, each can claim an extra $10 million in revenue to artificially inflate the revenue line on the P&L.

Not all businesses distort their financial statements, but given the chance most will use it to put their best corporate foot forward.

We were in the Louisville, Kentucky, office of Lantech's CFO, discussing accounting and financial reporting when Jean Cunningham with obvious frustration and red-hot feelings about the subject said, while waving a thick bunch of papers in the air, "Here, look at this if you want to see inconsistencies. Just this morning I was reviewing this credit risk report for a company whose name I won't mention. But you could pick any company, there's nothing special about this one." What seemed to increase the heat at the back of her neck was that "all reports seem to have the same inconsistencies."

This particular report, Jean complained, "says they lost 7.3 cents a share. Okay. Then, a paragraph later, it says they lost 0.35 cents a share. What gives? It's the same reporting period and two different numbers." She shook the pile of papers to emphasize her frustration.

But then Ms. Cunningham proceeded calmly to answer her own question. "This is how the financial statements are for every company. They're filled with special this, special that, extraordinary this and that. Because the way it's reported is so complicated, no one can understand . . . Forget about investing in them, you can't figure out if it's a good company, a bad company, worth lending to or even whether you should extend them open credit. You certainly can't tell if they're productive. It's all gobbledygook."

What's most appalling is that because of the vast resources

required to generate a detailed financial statement, many executives attach a reverence to the document. They reason: "Gee, if we spent that much money creating it then it must be right." The fact is that company leaders attempt to make operational decisions based on the contents of their financial statements. Even more frightening is when executives make operational decisions solely for the purpose of making the next financial statement more attractive than the last one. You'd have to be a modern-day Rip Van Winkle deep in slumber not to know how pervasive corporate exaggeration and in some instances chicanery have become with financial statements.

No company will become truly more productive by making decisions based on a historical document that's been massaged and manipulated in the interests of pleasing the analysts, delighting the loan officers and appeasing the shareholders while simultaneously minimizing tax liabilities, stroking the ego and putting another notch in the belt of the CEO.

A Little, Dark Secret

Along the way a simple skill set eludes most of us; some guys never learned how to throw a baseball, other people skipped learning about flossing until the dentist told them years later, and others never learned how to swim. Any admission, long after we imagined we were supposed to have mastered the skill, would be embarrassing. So, as prideful human beings, rather than admit what we consider to be a failing, we either avoid acknowledging what we don't know/can't do or fake it.

The truth is that the majority of business owners, managers and CEOs who weren't schooled in accounting and finance can't read a financial statement; they find most of the myriad lines on the statement to be gibberish. But rather than admit, they pretend—because they'd be too embarrassed to confess to landing in the top spot without being able to read a financial statement with any real finesse. Instead they're forced to rely on the help of a cadre of people who are prepared to become enablers—the business managers, head accountants and CFOs.

SRC's Jack Stack says that most CEOs receive their copy of the financial statement, put it in the safe, slam the door and say, "Okay, now we've got to design a new way of doing things," but never tell anybody what was in the documents. He says, "I came to the conclusion a long time ago that the reason executives lock up the financial information is because most of them don't understand it."

Deep down, people who can't interpret a financial statement know they can't, and the financial types around them have also caught on. Rather than remedy the situation they form an uneasy alliance where the accountant types patiently explain all the magical formulas, equations and ratios while the top gun nods and pretends to have known it all along. The more complicated the financial experts make their potions and formulas, the more important they become. In many businesses the accountants become the de facto operating heads of the enterprise as they tell the person in charge what to do and when to do it. The accountants end up with an inflated sense of self and the person in charge largely becomes a figurehead waiting to take her next cue from the business manager or CFO.

"What a Mess"

Simply connect the following dots and guess at the likely consequences.

If the financial statements used by most companies are never intended as anything more than historical statements of fact and not the basis for operating decisions; if they are just carefully spun fairy tales; and if most of the people who need them don't understand them anyway, then there's little wonder why most businesses fail.

And those that don't fail constantly struggle. No wonder only a few elite companies are ever able to become highly productive power-houses.

A highly productive company doesn't use a financial statement as a basis for leading and managing the business. It uses carefully selected Drivers to keep it moving forward and constantly becoming more productive.

The Drivers of Productivity

Notwithstanding their size, the companies we studied almost exclusively focus on a small number of important tasks and then work relentlessly to improve each of them, knowing that if they're successful the financial statement will ultimately reflect their success. (Rather than using the term "metric," which is a sad little leftover from the ultrahip vocabulary of the dotcom mania, and frequently used to refer to anything numerical, we'll strive to attach significance to the following tasks and will refer to them as Drivers.)

One company devoted to accounting that reports on productivity is Wiremold, a highly successful wire and cabling company and part of France's $3 billion Legrand Electric S.A. Wiremold has been practicing an approach for more than a decade—an approach that sums up the simplicity of measuring a company's Drivers rather than complex sets of numbers that make up a financial statement. Wiremold's former VP of finance Orest Fiume says, "Productivity is about the relationship between quantity of output versus the quantity of input. It's not a dollar-based measure. It's a quantity-based measure." He maintains that in order to make any accounting system relevant "the first thing you have to do is understand the importance of things being expressed in quantity, not in dollars. If you're trying to get people to focus on productivity and you try to express it in dollars, you're just going to confuse everyone."

One excellent example of using Drivers to lead and manage a business is the methods employed by Herb and Marion Sandler to power World Savings to success. The entire culture of the company is designed to focus attention on: deposit growth, mortgage origination, client retention and keeping general and administrative expenses extremely low. Concentrating exclusively on those few Drivers might not seem as sexy as getting your company in all kinds of risky and money-losing business propositions. The Sandlers often remind anyone who will listen that nineteen of the top twenty S&Ls from just fifteen years ago no longer exist. Concentrating on a few Drivers has paid off handsomely for World Savings, where more than five thousand workers share a nearly evangelical fervor for improving the numbers.

While most publicly traded companies engage in the murky practice of giving forward-looking advice to brokers, bankers, analysts and shareholders in the form of guidance, forecasting for the market what their future results will be, Herb Sandler disdains the practice. "We don't give guidance," he says; "we pay attention to measuring and improving those things that make us successful, and when we release our results everyone gets them at the same time."

At Nucor the Drivers are as decidedly unglamorous as those at World Savings. Each week each steel mill prepares a report that lists their order entry, sales backlogs, production and shipments and submits it to CEO Dan DiMicco for his review. Each factory in the Joist and Metals Building Group prepares a similar report that measures the numbers of quotes it has made, order entry, backlog, production and shipments. Everyone at Nucor clearly understands the numbers that drive productivity and demands that they be accurately measured and are constantly moving upward. As long as the company maintains low costs they know that profits, cash flow, earnings per share and a solid financial statement are the natural outcome.

Lantech's CFO Jean Cunningham asks, "How many financial

statements have you seen that tell you what your new orders are? None! How in the world can a company make a profit without new orders? They can't."

The big Drivers at Lantech include new orders, shipments and variable margin. "Our mantra around here," says Cunningham, "is if you don't ship it, you don't have income and you don't make a profit. All our shipments show gross profitability and you just can't do that with regular accounting."

SRC also uses Drivers to propel the company. As CEO Jack Stack describes it, when everyone at each of the plants gathers every Wednesday for a "no B.S." staff meeting, "the sessions are about the important numbers. You take your stories, convert them into a number, walk to the front of the room and write it down for everyone in the plant to see. What else do you really need in a staff meeting—right? That's all you need." SRC is a company where all the employees have been taught to understand the significance of every Driver that gets posted.

Orest Fiume stresses the importance of employing Drivers to make a business more productive when he says, "The numbers a company uses should be actionable. For example, we no longer calculate or publish a return on investment number because nobody, on a day-to-day basis, can figure out what to do to make it better. It's totally nonactionable."

Fiume follows up with some advice that seems hard to beat: "What you need are real numbers at lower levels of the organization that are actionable by people who have real jobs and do the real work."

The Drivers companies share in common are each quantity-based and delivered on either a real time, daily or weekly basis. None of the companies we studied relies on month-old data, interpreted by accountants who make decisions about the business proposition.

When a company finally creates a process where the things that truly drive a business, generate revenues and improve productivity are regularly measured, the financial statement becomes secondary. It is secondary in the sense that the other measurements being used give control of the business; the financial statements just confirm what you already know. When that happens, productivity will flourish.

A Word of Caution

If a company's objective is to dramatically increase productivity, it is a fact that it can learn from the most efficient companies in the world, which have already illuminated the way. The bottom line is to identify the key Drivers, measure them regularly and seek constant improvement. As obvious as the lessons may be and as easy as it might seem to implement these three precepts, any company that decides to begin leading and managing by utilizing Drivers will hear grumblings of protest from an unlikely source.

Most companies have too many people shuffling papers and entering transactions that in turn create reams of meaningless reports and documents, crammed with data useful primarily to defend past decisions instead of guiding future ones. This junk nobody is able to understand pacifies the data churners whose sense of importance will be lessened once things change. Expect them to protest.

Sounding one more alarm bell, Orest Fiume says, "I think people in the accounting profession could do a much better job of presenting information to people who don't have a degree in accounting. If they're unable to do that, a good case can be built that they're part of the waste."

Accountants and MBAs are trained to analyze dollars, and therefore financial statements are typically expressed in dollars. Fiume says that productivity is completely different. It is his view that the dollars on a financial statement are only the product of what's been sold multiplied by how many times you've sold it. According to Fiume, "The real costs aren't the dollars but the pounds of steel that were consumed times the price per pound, and the labor cost is the hours worked times the rate per hour paid." Because accountant types have been trained to produce and read statements composed only of dollars, Fiume holds the accountants responsible saying, "They often become a fundamental barrier to productivity."

Once highly productive companies have elected to use a series of Drivers to move their business forward the next obvious step is to turn each of the processes they measure into a system that can constantly be refined and improved. That's where we're headed in the next chapter.

9

Systematize Everything

Things want to flow and people want to flow. Most of the time we're tripped up by our own socks.

—Ed Constantine, Simpler Consulting

Highly productive companies have a system for *every* part of their business. And they work it over and over and over again.

The problem is that most people who view themselves as professionals think that systems are for blue-collar workers and don't apply to them.

As I worked on this chapter, struggling with a way to strongly emphasize the vital role that systems play in highly productive companies, I found myself on an airplane flying home from Atlanta.

Next to me sat the national sales manager for a big pharmaceutical company. I guessed he'd be an ideal candidate for a discussion about systems.

As his story developed, he proudly told me he had six regional sales managers and more than a hundred business development managers (salespeople) working for him, and he took me through his ascendancy up the rungs of his company.

"It must be hard keeping track of so many people," I said, playing dumb. "What kind of sales systems do you have in place?"

"That's a touchy subject," he said. "Years ago when I started in this business, I spent several years as a rep for another drug company, calling on doctors. They had so many systems I hated it.

"I promised myself," he continued, "that if I ever became a manager, I'd simply hire good people and set them loose to get the business. Sales types," he said, "don't like systems and don't like being told how to do things. That's why they're salespeople. They want to be free to do things how they want. As long as they don't break any laws," he winked, "I don't care how they get the business or what it takes."

Because his experiences with top-down systems had been bad, his answer was to set people free to do whatever they wanted.

A quick Internet search the next day revealed that $10,000 invested in his company five years previously was worth $6,200 while $10,000 invested in the overall pharmaceutical sector was worth $18,500. He either needed some systems . . . or better drugs.

Based on our research into productive enterprises, we came to two irrefutable facts: You can't improve a process until you have a system. And any business without systems where everybody is free to do their own thing is little more than an insane asylum run by the inmates.

What's a System?

Ten years ago, a young General Motors engineer who was in a master's program at Stanford defined productive systems as well as anyone ever has. We tracked Brent Hendrix down in Indiana, where he works as a production manager for Allison Transmission, a GM division, and discussed his definition.

"A system," Brent says, "is work in which the sequence of job elements has been efficiently organized and is repeatedly followed by a team member. The work sequence that is followed represents the 'best practices' involved in completing the job. The aim of a system is to reduce the variation introduced, thus eliminating waste and achieving high productivity. It's also the baseline of the continuous improvement philosophy in which the involvement of the team member is vital."

Hendrix's explanation makes the four most important points about systems:

1. Everyone does things the same way each time.
2. The company has determined that each step is the best way to perform the task.
3. The objective is to perform the task with zero variation.
4. The way a task is done becomes the baseline for continued improvement.

Highly productive companies turn virtually all aspects of their business into systems.

Whether it's the way Ryanair sells tickets (on its Web site and over the phone but not through travel agents), the way Lantech builds machines (one at a time), the way World Savings appraises houses (with its own appraisers and time-honed formulas), the way IKEA ships furniture or the way every single task is completed at Yellow's freight centers, each method has made a successful process into a system that can be steadily improved.

Systems at Work

Let's look at the way World Savings manages budgeting. Like most businesses, it has a rigorous budget process in which targets and costs are projected for the coming year and each proposed expenditure is subjected to the famous Marion Sandler question, WTGBRFDT. But she says, "No matter how accurate your budgets are, there are those inevitable occasions when you need to spend money that wasn't in the budget."

A department manager has some wiggle room or perhaps has built in an amount for contingencies that are not budgeted. But what happens when businesses must confront proposed expenditures that are too big for the amount of wiggle they built in or too great for the contingency fund? Someone eventually has to make a judgment call "to spend or not to spend." Generally that decision falls on the shoulders of the business owner, CEO or a very senior executive, someone with the power of the pen. Not so at World Savings.

"Our *system* for handling items not covered in our approved budget is to present each of them to our budget review committee," says Sandler. One might immediately imagine a committee of white-haired, experienced old-timers nodding together in condescension as they listen patiently to the pleas and woes of budget ailments and requests for dollars.

Not so at World Savings. What makes its budget review committee unique is that the company uses membership on the committee as a way of quickly indoctrinating staff and executives into the World Savings culture.

Sandler describes the committee as a rotating one that was conceived also as an excellent way for people to learn how the company thinks and operates. "By changing membership, we provide more of our people an opportunity to experience and truly understand our culture."

What's most surprising about the budget review committee at World is that neither of the Sandlers, the firm's co-CEOs, sit on the committee. "I've been a member in the past and so has Herb," Marion says, "but you have to understand that we're a family here. We have many very talented people here and we trust them." Simply having a committee to review proposed spending outside the budget constitutes a system by taking it out of the hands of a single "important" person.

Recognizing that you can't improve productivity without standardized systems, Yellow Corp.'s Bill Zollars decided his company needed to implement systems across all the company's hundreds of terminals. Zollars says, "No sooner had I arrived than I realized the company was full of good people trying to do the right thing but there were as many processes as there were terminals."

According to Zollars, Yellow started from scratch on a search for best practices involving the people who actually performed the work. He says, "We took apart every process, every system and finally determined the best way to perform each task."

Zollars selected the company's huge Cleveland terminal as the first location for implementation. At first employees fought the new systems, believing they were just another way for management to snoop on them. But the Cleveland plant manager, Rick Brenneman, persevered, eventually got everyone onboard and made the program a huge success and then watched as productivity increased dramatically.

Next Zollars directed that the firm's largest one hundred terminals implement the new systems for pickup and delivery. Once those systems were implemented the terminal would earn Silver Certification and begin work toward Gold Certification, which included systems for dock processes and line-haul operations. In order to make certain that each plant understood participation wasn't an option the company dispatched a team composed of an area general manager, a terminal manager and an industrial engineer to each plant for seven weeks to coach and guide them to certification.

The results were predictable. As terminals achieved Silver and then Gold status hundreds of millions of dollars in inefficiencies were driven out of the company's costs and productivity soared.

You'll also recall that everyone who works for SRC's twenty-two companies gathers once a week in their respective lunchrooms and takes part in a review of the business's financial performance for the previous week. By doing it week-in week-out for many years the exercise has also become a system. We'd imagined it would take hours for the people responsible for the various lines of the P&L and balance sheet to walk to the front of the room, fill in the blank they're responsible for and furnish a brief explanation.

"No way," says Jack Stack, smiling. "When you do it every week, over and over again, and everyone has learned the game of business, it doesn't take much time at all. Everyone comes to the front of the room, writes in their number and makes a quick comment.

"It's a system," Stack says, "and it moves fast. People have learned not to waste time making excuses—the numbers are the numbers. And others have learned not to give people a hard time because the next week they might be up there writing down a number *they're* not proud of."

Consider the results of performing the same task or function over and over and over again, always doing it the same way, yet trying each time to do it faster, better, more economically, and constantly gathering input from everyone involved. You not only have a system, you have one that will inevitably result in increased productivity.

People Fight the "S" Word

We wondered why most enterprises have limited the introduction of systems to the factory floor, allowing other areas of the company to do their own thing.

"There's absolutely no good reason that systems aren't applicable in every part of the business," claims Chairman Pat Lancaster of Lantech. "It's just that the whole world is accustomed to screwing with the shop floor. Every new engineer from MIT and all the Harvard MBAs think they've got the big, new answer for fixing the factory. And there seems to be a pervasive feeling that while people on the shop floor can be messed with, other departments are sacred cows."

Bruce Thompson and Ed Constantine of the Simpler Consulting

Group agree that all areas of a business should operate with systems that encourage work to move along a natural and dependable path.

Seasoned consultants like Bruce and Ed agree that people generally behave according to practices that may have come out of some management decision—using hazy methods that were probably decided in some reengineering exercise.

Thompson says, "Most companies have developed into a norm culture where ten years ago someone made a mistake with a purchase order and a process was put into place that POs had to be approved twice." He smiles as he describes what often happens. "The person's been gone for years, the company has added new technology that wouldn't allow that error to be made again, but the company still has people running around getting multiple approvals on purchase orders."

Although circumstances constantly change, Constantine observes that "most companies don't change the process to reflect the new circumstances. The net result is that you have all these departments processing stuff only because it's always been done that way and the workers fiercely defend what they do because they don't want to lose their jobs."

Pat Lancaster warns, "You'd better be ready when you go into any department other than the factory floor and try to implement a system, because the first thing you'll hear is, 'Mess with my job, buster, and I'm out of here.'"

We think Jim Womack of the Lean Enterprise Institute edges even closer to the real reason people fight systems. Jim says, "One of the big problems you have to confront is people who consider themselves 'professionals' and think that what professionals do is make one-off big decisions all day long, which is another way of saying they think their job is to be important and reinvent the wheel every day."

Whittling Away the Edges

The people who lead highly productive companies are all strong people, clear in their resolve of how the business will be run. By contrast, many other business executives are so seemingly afraid to rock the boat, offend anyone or tread on anybody's space that nothing of substance ever changes. It's one cosmetic initiative after another.

An event that occurred in my consulting practice illustrates the point. A large company hired me to help improve the fortunes of their very cumbersome sales department. The day I showed up at the company with several members of the consulting team a veteran sales executive met us at the front door. With hair wildly flying, eyes blazing and arms waving to deny us entry, she was like the mad woman of Chaillot.

"I know what you people do," she screamed, "you turn everybody into robots with your f—ing systems. We'll, it's not going to happen here. We're not having any [lots of expletives deleted] systems here. If you take one step inside this door the entire sales department is going to walk out and quit and put this place out of business."

As her rant continued I hoped she didn't have a gun or a knife. It took a couple of her workmates to calm her down. Eventually she was led away while two others stood watchfully at the door.

My team decided to wait a few minutes to see if a new drama would unfold.

In a few moments the CEO who'd hired us appeared at the door. Ushering us out to the parking lot and with a very nervous smile on his face, he said, "Sorry about that. Remember, I told you we'd have a little resistance."

He mumbled as he looked for the right words. "Ah, why don't you go back to your hotel, I'll try to work things out and we'll meet at your place later today."

We had six hours to wonder what we'd gotten ourselves into. Later that evening, the CEO kicked off the discussion by saying, "I think I've got everything worked out so you folks can begin your work tomorrow. But I had to make a few concessions."

He looked down like someone who knows they're about to say something really dumb and hopes the other person is too dumb to notice. "Well," he said, "here's what the sales department wants."

Now, this was a company in serious trouble because of faltering sales and diminishing market share. Time was running out. If he wasn't able to get things fixed, revenues would continue to deteriorate, the stock price would continue to fall and eventually his head would be lopped off. Those were the very reasons we were hired.

"I'm sorry about the woman who gave you so much trouble today; she's been with the company a long time and doesn't like change."

"But," he continued, "she's a pretty good producer and we'd like to keep her if we can." He explained that she'd always been a troublemaker but that he didn't want her to diminish our chance of success. So he offered a compromise: "We'll separate her and a few others who always go along with her, give them a separate office and let them do things the way they've always done them."

"And . . . ?" I asked.

"There is one more thing." He was digging an even deeper hole for himself. "Most of the other people know we're in bad shape and need help and are willing to give things a try . . . on one condition."

"And what would that condition be?" I wondered aloud.

He hesitated. "Well, if you and your team suggest anything that any of them doesn't want to do, each wants the right not to use that part."

You can guess what eventually happened to that company.

Managers who are preoccupied with pleasing everyone, offending no one and prepared to compromise everything they believe in are incapable of adopting and implementing the systems required to lead a company to increased productivity.

Management must be prepared for resistance to systems because:

- Some workers will be so resentful over the imposition of systems that they'll do almost anything in their power to stop them.
- Some people think their education or professional status puts them above the use of a system.
- Others simply don't want any part of anything that might measure their productivity.

Whatever their length of time on the job, most workers have seen lots of harebrained initiatives that disrupt their work, then founder and sink . . . only to be replaced by a new fad initiative that comes in with the next tide. No wonder workers roll their eyes in disbelief at the manager's latest discovery. They mumble to themselves and to each other that the boss should "get real," digging in their heels while pretending to embrace this "newest, latest and best" program for efficiency. The top-down imposition of any system communicates clearly to workers that management thinks they, the workers, are too stupid to figure out a better way of doing their tasks. When you add the fact that layoffs have always been a result of both management's blunders and increased productivity, you have a potentially incendiary environment.

On the other hand, the financial performance of most companies is tracked hour-to-hour and day-by-day by investors, bankers, analysts, the stock market and the financial press. One hiccup can spell professional disaster for an executive or a PR nightmare for the company. Many managers, executives and business owners are so fearful of disrupting the applecart that they passively turn control of the enterprise over to the workers.

Instead of having standardized systems and processes, many managers, owners and executives have instead jumped to the other end of the spectrum and proclaimed that their business has "empowered" the workers. The term is used so frequently that it has achieved buzzword status. Productivity experts think that the way the word is used is hogwash. What too often results is a chaotic mess that is impossible to control or measure.

Empowerment Can Be a Big Excuse for Doing Nothing

The employees of highly successful companies are empowered, but in highly productive ways. They're empowered:

- To do things the way they and their colleagues have determined to be best practices.
- To work continually to improve those best practices.
- To conduct themselves according to the values and mores of the company culture.

The employees play as much a role as management in deciding what the systems will be. That's real empowerment.

Trust and Respect Are Required for Systems to Work

The reason many companies have so much trouble introducing systems boils down to two words—words that are, in fact, the basis of any worthwhile relationship: trust and respect.

If management doesn't trust and respect the workers and the workers don't trust and respect the management, the company cannot become truly productive. Until a manager, executive, business owner or CEO figures out how to solve the issue, any increase in productivity the organization might experience is likely to be short-lived.

Trust and respect don't happen when management extols the importance of its workforce and then announces major layoffs. They don't happen when the leaders loot the corporate coffers for extravagant perks and privilege. They definitely don't happen when consultants with pained looks on their faces are needed to tell the people at the top how to do their jobs.

When a company doesn't possess the high level of trust and respect that exists between people at companies like Nucor, World Savings, IKEA, SRC and Lantech, its stuck with a real conundrum.

The heads of business units demonstrate true respect and trust for the workers by actively soliciting their ideas and input. If they do, they're repaid by workers willing to contribute ideas and work harder, smarter, faster and more efficiently toward the goal of helping the enterprise win.

Until mutual trust and respect is demonstrated within organizations, the result at best will be an uneasy impasse. A status quo will exist—same stuff, different day. Lots of meetings. Many urgent decisions to be made and fires to be put out. Continually reinventing the wheel. No effective productivity measures. Flocks of self-important peacocks in polished black wing tips strutting around making grand pronouncements. But unfortunately, there will be no significant increase in productivity and a continuation of management's never-ending search for a magic bullet or the latest alphabet-soup management theory.

Building trust and respect depends on interpersonal skills well worth learning if one is to succeed at managing a productive organization. (Or succeed in maintaining a satisfying relationship.)

Is It a Culture or a System?

It's not easy getting companies to cooperate in book projects. Who needs the bother of opening their calendar, company and financials to the scrutiny of a journalist or writer who might get it all wrong? You can imagine my reaction when at my computer one afternoon I found the following e-mail from Dan DiMicco at Nucor.

"Jason, you missed the entire point."

Kerplunk.

Ask Nucor's DiMicco about systems at his company and he might give you as blunt an answer as he gave me.

"The culture is the system and the system is the culture. Period."

He wasn't being smug. He's convinced that without a culture a company has nothing, and that no number of systems can give any business an edge in productivity unless they first have a culture.

In highly productive companies the culture is the system. And a series of systems form the culture.

The culture is based on:

- A set of deeply held values
- A sequence of work that has been efficiently organized and sys-temized
- An environment where the work follows "best practices" as deter-mined by those involved in completing the job
- A shared collective ambition to eliminate waste and the achieve-ment of high productivity, and
- A competitive environment where every act performed serves as a baseline for continuous improvement.

Our conclusion: Highly productive companies prove the proposi-tion that *Less Is More* by turning essential functions into systems and performing them over and over again, constantly driving out waste and striving for improvement. Until a company systematizes and has a standardized process for paying the bills, dealing with vendors and customers, selling its wares, producing its widgets and making deci-sions, increased productivity will remain wishful thinking.

During the course of our research we were sometimes led places we hadn't expected to go and learned lessons we didn't anticipate being taught. That's what happened when we discovered that the process one company used to consistently and dramatically increase its productivity was in fact used by all the other companies in the book, even though most didn't know they were doing it. To them it was just common sense. You'll find out what we learned in the next chapter.

10

Continuous Improvement

Anything that doesn't add value is waste. Good business managers have an obligation to constantly eliminate it.

—Pat Lancaster, chairman, Lantech

In their infancies, a few of the leading companies identified in our study were compelled to do more with less because financial resources were in short supply (SRC, The Warehouse and Ryanair). Others (World Savings, Nucor and IKEA) did more with less because of a set of guiding principles fiercely held by their founders; an abhorrence of waste, respect for the competitive spirit, an adherence to long-term strategies when making decisions and a strong commitment to the value of the individual people in their workforce.

When each of these highly productive companies initially achieved some financial victory, their leaders were smart enough to realize that being more productive than their rivals represented their sole competitive advantage. They reacted quickly and aggressively and moved to memorialize and institutionalize the values and systems—establishing cultures that propelled them to achieve greater success. There was a tacit understanding from the start that unless they remained more productive than the competition, they could quickly lose their competitive advantage. Their leaders took nothing for granted.

For each of these companies, continuous improvement and a dedication to becoming continuously more efficient was simply doing what came *naturally* in a business world where such behavior is quite *unnatural*. (I call this *unnatural* because there have been untold hundreds of thousands of enterprises that experienced early success from the same creativity, ingenuity and productivity but promptly veered off course and crashed and burned the moment they enjoyed even modest financial success.)

For Yellow Corp. and Lantech, the journey to continuous improvement occurred another way. Both were once highly successful enterprises whose fortunes had been protected by government regulation (Yellow) and patents (Lantech). Both companies faced bleak and uncertain futures when deregulation occurred in the trucking business and when Lantech's inventions lost their patent protection.

You've already read how Bill Zollars took the helm at Yellow and embarked on a daring course when he promptly off-loaded the majority of the executives, brought in a diverse leadership team from outside the trucking industry, and took the company out of the trucking business and transformed it into a transportation solutions business.

Pat Lancaster of Lantech chose another equally bold path, one that provides a startling model for any company needing to quickly become more productive. The more we studied the results at Lantech, the more apparent it became that all of the principles behind Pat Lancaster's course of action are practiced by all the other highly productive companies we researched, even though none of the others calls it by the same name. We concluded that no company has a chance to truly become more productive, or to continually improve the products or services they offer, without embracing these same principles.

Lancaster chose *kaizen*—a process known by several other names including "lean manufacturing," "just-in-time manufacturing" and the "Toyota method." Whatever it's called or whatever spin the consultants put on it, the principles behind *kaizen* echo simple common sense. All highly productive companies committed to continual improvement practice some version of it.

What's *Kaizen*?

The word *kaizen,* translated from Japanese as "continuous improvement," first surfaced here in the 1970s when American industry started getting its collective butt kicked by Japan—never realizing that America's own industrial philosophers had jump-started the concept.

More than one hundred years ago, Henry Ford was actively developing one of the world's first mass production systems to improve productivity. Driven by a gut level goal to get the price of a car down to where the person building it could afford to buy one, Ford worked simultaneously on many different techniques, including interchangeable parts, production lines and standard processes. He concentrated his thinking on perfecting mass production—a process that ultimately resulted in reducing the price of a car from seven hundred dollars to less than three hundred dollars.

In the late 1920s, a Japanese businessman named Taiichi Ohno visited Henry Ford to see how companies in the United States were using mass production. Ohno's primary discovery was that Ford had been successful at reducing the time it took to manufacture an automobile from seven hundred minutes to less than ninety.

During Ohno's trip he also visited American supermarkets, then unknown in Japan. He was keenly impressed by the way food was stacked on shelves and replaced only as needed, and it provided him with a fascinating insight that would aid the development of Japanese manufacturing. Unlike the situation in the United States, where Ford had access to plentiful capital for buying materials ahead of time, and lots of room to pile up massive inventories, in Japan space and raw materials were short. Ohno realized the tremendous financial savings that could result from not stockpiling parts in inventory.

Just a couple of years later the people at Toyota, a company that had been in the weaving and loom business, started manufacturing automobiles for the Japanese government using the techniques Ohno had observed while visiting the United States. He put together Ford's ideas with the just-in-time inventory idea gleaned from supermarkets, and the early writings of another American, Frederick Taylor. Things were going very well for Ohno and Toyota when all hell broke loose with World War II, and every Japanese company found itself either bankrupt or about to go bankrupt. Toyota, desperate to stay in business, began importing the ideas of another American consultant, W. Edwards Deming, whose recommendations about quality control and statistical quality had been blithely rejected by American industry.

Finally in the late 1960s Toyota put all the pieces together, and the idea of *kaizen* was formally introduced. The Toyota people extended an offer of lifelong employment on the condition that employees would use the innovative techniques that made their jobs easier, faster, better and more quality oriented. Management insisted on their full participation in driving out waste. The results were nothing short of spectacular and the Japanese companies that embraced *kaizen* routinely become dramatically more productive than their American competitors.

The greatest irony is that in 1979, Ford, Inc.—where it all actually began—decided to purchase part of Mazda to learn how to apply the principles of *kaizen*.

Shut 'er Down Folks . . . We're Starting Over!

When Lantech lost their Supreme Court battle over the patents that had protected and ensured their success, Pat Lancaster knew that modest improvements in manufacturing, sales and customer service wouldn't be sufficient, that radical changes had to be made fast. His company had to immediately become more productive.

Recognizing he needed help, Lancaster hired Anand Sharma, CEO of TBM Consulting Group and a man named by *Fortune* magazine as one of America's Heroes of Manufacturing, to "*kaizen*" his factory.

The classic *kaizen* exercise is done in five days and is often called a *kaizen* blitz or breakthrough. Within only a few days the people involved build a set of objectives for increased productivity, map the current processes, collectively design the new ones and immediately implement the new processes.

Lancaster started the *kaizen* exercise by completely shutting down the old assembly line and ceremoniously turning off the computerized IBM MRP (material requirements planning) system that his company had invested millions of dollars in. "We had forty people involved in the exercise," says Lancaster, "and there was no going back to where we'd been. We were trapped into going forward."

Anand Sharma says he takes special delight at the end of the second day of a five-day *kaizen*. "As soon as we've set the productivity objectives, mapped out the old process and determined what the new process will be, I wait for the question to be asked, 'When do we implement this stuff?'"

At that point Sharma tells them that the time for talking is over and it's time for action. "Let's do it right now! We're not going to spend any huge money making changes," he announces, "and if something doesn't work, we'll fix it." He emphasizes that the effort will involve creativity before capital, and quick and crude rather than slow and elegant.

Lancaster remembers it as an incredible experience when everyone worked twenty hours a day and nobody went home. "We took a small space in our huge manufacturing facility, scrubbed the floor and said, 'This will be our new factory' and went to work building the new assembly facility." Over the next two days, the forty members of the team constructed a new temporary facility out of cardboard, wood and whatever was required, and then began manufacturing.

One story that Lancaster tells makes a powerful point not only about his experiences with his company's quest for increased productivity and continual improvement but one that speaks to a personality trait we saw exhibited by all the leaders of highly productive companies: zero ego. He explains that in any organization really committed to continuous improvement, the people have a say but the *establishment* doesn't (we found this uncommon trait shared by every single company we researched). "So although I was part of the process," Lancaster says, "I was there not as the company CEO but as a team member dressed in jeans and working alongside everyone else."

He worked with a small team assigned the job of building a temporary turntable out of wood that would be essential in the new manufacturing process. "I had this vision for what it should look like and convinced my team. So we went to work building it and what we built was slick. When we finished, it was ten o'clock at night; we were grubby, sweating like pigs and really excited as we prepared to show the whole team what we'd built. It was cool beyond belief.

"What we didn't know," he says, "is that another small team was working on another version of a turntable. And when both were presented to the entire team, it became obvious that the other one was better than ours. To this day the entire company still talks about the night they put the boss's design in the Dumpster."

Lancaster says that what occurs during a *kaizen* blitz "serves as a forming image for any company getting set to commit to continuous improvement. The guy that owns the place, the top dog that runs the place, is not only *not* right all the time but can also be confronted when he's wrong. The beauty of *kaizen* is that the merit of the alternatives decides things, not rank," he insists.

"We started our *kaizen* on a Monday," says Lancaster, "and had to have the new facility up and running by Thursday night so we could start production on Friday. For four days we had chaos with people running trying to get the new system built." The timetable seemed impossible, yet, he says, everyone knew "We'd get it done."

By the end of that week, Lantech was building machines according to the new process—one at a time—to fulfill the six orders they averaged each day, no more and no less. Today the vast and sparkling-clean Lantech facility is home to eight small factories within the building, each producing error free exactly the number of machines that have been sold each day.

Lancaster says, "There's nothing that can't be made more productive within a week." He adds, "It's through our constant focus on continuous improvement and letting demand totally drive supply that we were able to triple sales with the same size staff, reduce from five weeks to eleven hours the time required to manufacture a machine, and increase productivity one percent per month for seven years."

All Highly Productive Companies Employ the Same Principles for Continuous Improvement

To the certain protest of many *kaizen* practitioners who would have you believe there's either something complex or magical about *kaizen*, our study and research led us to conclude there are seven readily identifiable steps involved in continuous improvement. Here is the way all the companies we studied continually improve what they do—even if they've never heard of *kaizen*.

Leadership must be involved in continuous improvement

One of the vital components of *kaizen* is something called *genchi genbutsu,* which translates as "go, see, be involved." We witnessed this in practice at every company we studied. The management of companies committed to continuous improvement spends far more time on the line, in the stores, with the workers and with customers than do the executives of most companies.

Bob Rosinski, senior partner with Anitech Inc., a *kaizen* consulting firm, has implemented *kaizen* over 250 times in companies varying from an aerospace engineering firm to a casino. He attests that, without fail, management buy-in is the most important step in the *kaizen* process. "There have been instances where lean manufacturing *kaizen* deployments have failed," he admits. "But you can almost always trace it to a lack of management commitment, a lack of management involvement, or just kind of a *laissez faire* attitude from management where they delegate it down into the organization somewhere."

Whether it's Dan DiMicco visiting every Nucor facility annually, answering his own phone and responding to every employee e-mail, Bill Zollars on an eighteen-month-long odyssey of hundreds of Yellow locations and thousands of meetings with employees, or Jack Stack knowing the name of all of SRC's one thousand plus workforce and being able to explain the purpose of every piece of equipment in each of their twenty-two factories, the people who lead organizations committed to continuous improvement are expert practitioners of going, seeing and being involved. They understand that continuous improvement is about the ongoing elimination of waste and that in most cases they alone have the authority to approve the resources, eliminate out-of-date practices and procedures, and initiate or okay the sweeping changes required to become more productive. Companies whose bosses sit on their bums in plush offices don't become highly productive.

There's agreement on the objectives

Each of the companies we studied has determined the important Drivers that propel its business, and then systematically involved everyone in the formulation of specific productivity targets to improve those metrics.

These Drivers are *not* items shown on a financial statement. In the case of Ryanair, the Drivers are turnaround time of airplanes, the food and merchandise sold onboard, the hotel rooms and rental cars booked, on-time performance and load factors. At World Savings the Drivers are deposit growth, mortgage origination growth, client retention, customer satisfaction and maintaining extraordinarily low G&A (general and administrative) expenses. At Nucor the primary Driver is the tons of steel produced per team, per hour, and at The Warehouse the Drivers are margin, inventory turns and customer satisfaction.

People whose personality types aren't suited to an environment of continuous improvement and constant measurement either aren't hired by highly productive companies or quickly decide—frequently helped along by fellow team members—that the culture isn't right for them.

Highly productive companies understand that continuous improvement is intentional; it doesn't happen by accident and if it's going to be achieved there must be agreed-upon objectives and they must be measured.

You need to know what the real product or service is

Pat Lancaster of Lantech says that when he decided to *kaizen* his company, "We were making three different products at the same time and what we discovered was that those three products had more to do with our history as a company than with what our clients wanted or needed."

Lancaster remembers, "We started the company with a single product and as time went on we tweaked it and made it better. Then, we'd introduce the one that was better but keep the old because we thought it had a loyal following. When we became committed to continuous improvement we were forced to address that insanity as part of the process. We quickly realized the absurdity of having three similar models targeting essentially the same market."

James Womack, author of the 1990s hit book *The Machine That Changed the World,* says that "Figuring out what their real product is confuses lots of business people." But he is quick to share a tip: "Ask the question 'What's our real product or service?' completely from the perspective of the customer." He says that without a definitive answer, increased productivity and continuous improvement can't get off the ground.

Bob Rosinski couldn't agree more with Womack's customer focused approach. "The whole idea is to move the business, or the department, or the production line, or the office area, or whatever it is, toward more of a just-in-time environment, so that they're thinking what their customer wants, when their customer wants it, in the quantity the customer wants, with perfect quality, and only doing those things that the customer is willing to pay for," he says emphatically, and short of breath. And we couldn't agree with Rosinski more. What's the point of unnecessary steps if it doesn't help the customer?

Womack insists that there is an absolute need to start by determining what the real product is of each work group. Employees participating in the continuous improvement process experience what Womack describes as "a powerfully positive psychological effect when they discover what the concrete product of their department, business unit, or company is, be it physical or digital. The psychological effect begins to kick in when employees start thinking, 'Hey, you know, I really am making something. I really am producing a sale, I'm really producing something tangible that will benefit someone.'"

Start by mapping the current process

A company can't improve a process unless it can first identify it as a process that needs to be improved.

Jean Cunningham, Lantech's CFO, used yarn to map out all the back office and accounting functions on a big board. She says the end result of mapping all the back office processes was a "joke" and she and her team were able to more than double their efficiency simply by eliminating all the stops, twists and turns that slowed everything down. Whether it's approving a mortgage at World Savings, bending a piece of steel at Nucor, unloading appliances off a truck at The Warehouse or selling an airplane ticket online at Ryanair you can't improve a process and make it more productive until you can see the current process.

Bob Rosinski related to us the process of building a map to locate waste. "This is a map that simply indicates where the various processes are that touch the product from raw material to the customer, or even in a service environment, from the inception of an order to the completion of that order." In other words, you figure out how many twists, turns, roundabout paths, and unnecessary steps your product takes before it reaches the customer.

Anand Sharma, who engineered the transformation of Lantech into a model of productivity, uses an unexpected food metaphor when he likens the work flow at most companies to a pot of boiling pasta. "You map out the flow of work and production at most companies and you'll end up with a pot of spaghetti. But instead of simplifying things," he says, "most companies opt for complex computer systems to try and track and stay on top of things." According to Sharma, the net effect "is like putting a blanket on top of the problem and ending up with automated waste." He warns that most computer systems merely let you know a little faster how badly you're really doing.

If you try to map out a business unit's process to find the way things are getting done from start to finish and you find it impossible to create the map, you've just uncovered the root cause of the unit's inefficiency. Creating a system to identify and understand the way things are actually being done sets the stage for the next step, which is about improvement.

The people performing the work must be involved in the new process

Pat Lancaster says that before a company can improve something, everyone has to really understand waste. When someone who's thought about it a bit is asked what waste is, he says they'll probably answer something like, "Waste is stuff that's damaged in shipment or stuff that you make wrong and have to throw away." But that definition misses an essential idea. And if it stands as a company's definition of waste, the elimination of true waste becomes nearly impossible.

Lancaster adds some specifics: "Have people walk though a factory, office or retail showroom floor and observe what's not adding value. That's real waste. The best thing to do is the spaghetti diagram. And when you see that people have walked extra thousands of feet, back-tracked dozens of times, many people have touched the same piece of paper or multiple people have to approve something then you've found waste." He adds another point: "Anytime you're producing something in batches and end up generating inventory that's standing still, you've found even more waste." And nobody is better positioned to determine where real waste exists than the people actually performing the work.

In his book *Plain Talk,* Ken Iverson, the man who guided Nucor for thirty-one years, provides an excellent example of the principles behind *kaizen* in action at a company that doesn't know it's using it. He wrote, "We started a crew on a straightener machine—which straightens steel angles to meet customer requirements—at a production bonus baseline of eight tons per hour. The rated capacity of the machine was ten tons per hour. Well, that crew kept tinkering and experimenting trying to make it produce more. They installed a larger motor, fed the angles into the machine in various ways and so on. Within a year, their production was up to twenty tons an hour—twice that machine's rated capacity." Nucor's workers understood that waste isn't only poorly produced steel but slow motors, bad angling and wasted footsteps.

The improved process is implemented immediately

One of the guiding philosophies of *kaizen* is quick implementation of improved processes. We found this same commitment to fast action in the companies we studied. While most companies struggle with "paralysis by analysis" and nothing ever changes, in companies committed to continuous streamlining and efficiency, the GO button gets pushed the moment the WTGBRFDT question is answered.

Continuous improvement becomes the ethos of the company

In the opening paragraphs of this chapter I wrote that each of the companies we studied understood that unless it remained more productive than the competition, it could easily lose the competitive advantage it had worked so hard to achieve.

Every business that defies the odds and survives its first few tumultuous years (four out of five new businesses fail within the first three) is provided a clear choice. It can stick to its knitting and work relentlessly to improve its competitive advantage by becoming smarter and faster; building, producing and delivering for less; constantly working to reduce overheads; and fully using the human capital that's been entrusted to it. Or it can allow the dark forces to delude it into believing that the rules of the marketplace don't apply to it and that competitive advantage is its anointed right.

Scores of airlines have come and gone while Ryanair flies eleven million people per year, with designs on forty million by 2010. Woolworth is a distant memory, as are the Automat and many of the more recent dazzling Silicon Valley dotcoms. But the financial performance of The Warehouse continually improves.

Deregulation and the ensuing nightmare in the transportation business caused a lot of names to disappear while Yellow Corp. got better and better. Home Federal, Great American, Franklin and all the other names on the list of the top twenty S&Ls a decade ago got sopped up, merged away or went out of business while the fortunes of World Savings improve with each reporting period. And while one steel company after another either bites the dust or visits Washington, D.C., with a hat in its hand to beg the government to protect it and take over its pension liabilities, Nucor just keeps making steel and money.

Each of these productive companies understands that without a distinctive competitive advantage, market leadership is almost always fleeting. And it understands that unless it remains committed to a course of continual improvement, it will lose its edge.

Have The Warehouse, Nucor, Yellow Corp., IKEA, Ryanair, SRC and World Savings joined Lantech in the formal practice of *kaizen* as a management technique? No.

But do each of these companies practice every philosophical tenet of *kaizen?* A resounding yes! They do it through their mastery of:

- Leadership involvement in continuous improvement
- The setting of specific productivity objectives
- Maintaining a laser-sharp focus from the *customers'* perspective on the product or services they offer
- The constant mapping of current processes
- Involving the people who perform the actual work in the creation of new processes
- Fast implementation, and
- A relentless commitment to continual improvement.

Even though it might not know the *kaizen* word *muda* (waste), each of these companies would be a feather in the caps of Henry Ford, W. Edwards Deming, Frederick Taylor and even Taiichi Ohno.

How do some of the world's most productive companies pay people? Commissions? Bonuses? Or a carrot on the end of a stick? We found some differences but we also discovered some surprising similarities in the compensation plans of the highly productive companies, and that's where we're headed next.

11

Compensation

The man who does not work for the love of work but only for money is not likely to make money nor find much fun in life.

—Steel executive Charles M. Schwab

"Where do you think the universe ends?" mumbled one of my summer camp buddies.

I was eight or nine years old, groggy from too much sun and too much water and very sleepy. But on that night, as my eyelids drooped, I would be motivated to ask the question that would lead me to learn my first five-syllable word.

Our "after lights out" ritual was always dependably and comfortingly the same. First came the requisite round of ghost stories and then a series of mournful, eerie sounds created by teenage counselors lurking about outside our cabin. They seemed to find perverted pleasure in scaring the younger campers. To turn off our overactive youthful imaginations, my cabin mates and I would lie still in our bunks and one by one we would doze off while others would talk about weird intellectual stuff—youthful attempts at pondering the meaning of life.

This one particular night, following a few moments of heavy thinking, someone said, "The universe doesn't end, stupid. It goes on forever."

"It has to end somewhere," a voice countered from the dark.

"No, it doesn't," said another sure and determined voice.

"Does, too!"

"Does not . . ."

On and on it went. Finally, after many opinions were sounded, everyone fell asleep. I wasn't that lucky. This particular question kept me awake and vaguely troubled. I wondered whether the universe really ended and if it did intend to end, I was concerned about what the heck was keeping it from happening.

The next morning I sought out one of the adult counselors for an explanation. After listening to my question and thinking about it for a moment, he said, "Well, Jason, that's one of life's little *imponderables*."

I dashed to the small library, grabbed the moldy dictionary and sounded the word out over and over again as I looked up, *im-pon-der-a-ble*. I still remember the precise definition. "That which cannot be assessed in any definite way."

The Big Imponderable

Over these years as a business owner and consultant, I've observed that most companies seem more perplexed by the issue of how to pay people than I was with my "universe" question. Compensation plans have become the imponderables of big business.

The questions go on and on, seemingly without end: Should a company pay salespeople salaries or commissions, and how much? What about the merits of individual incentives versus group bonuses for production workers? Should people be paid upon sales or upon collections; and if upon sales, what's the impact on cash flow? Should employees be paid bonuses weekly, monthly, quarterly or annually? What about the role of stock options as a way of holding top performers? Hardly an issue of the *Harvard Business Review* goes by without a new theory on the imponderable subject of pay, bonuses and options.

To assist this never-ending quest for the perfect compensation plan, thousands of high-priced consultants are hired to tell companies how to pay their people. An army of experts stands ready to unveil their most recently tweaked and "processed" pay plan recommendations. Human resource specialists always manage to participate; they stay armed with deathly verbose studies, charts, graphs and PowerPoint presentations that bore a company's leadership until paralysis of thought is inevitable.

Almost every business meeting or convention features workshops with bold, promising titles like BRAND NEW EZ WAYS TO COMPENSATE. Unfortunately, the brilliant promise sputters to nothing when attendees find they are being subjected to hackneyed versions of the same old, same old. And if you should head for the hotel bar after a conference and listen in on the conversations, you're likely to hear many animated and heated discussions about the same subject. Next time you attend a conference, I predict you'll see folks already on their third Scotch busily using cocktail napkins to illustrate the wonder of their personal version of the "perfect" pay plan.

Toss into the mix the growing number of experts with theories on pay plans, including theoreticians like Alfie Kohn, the author of *No Contest: The Case Against Competition,* who argues that "individual rewards only succeed in gaining temporary compliance and just like punishment are strikingly ineffective." And so the long list of questions about how to pay people increases. Imponderable becomes *IMPONDERABLE.*

Dr. Jeffrey Pfeffer, author of many business books and currently the Thomas D. Dee II Professor of Organizational Behavior at the Stanford University Graduate School of Business, says, "It's easier for people to tinker with compensation than it is to address the real issue, the need to build a culture based on respect and trust."

In Pfeffer's view, "There are all these consulting firms that get hired to design compensation programs for businesses wanting to improve productivity. And of course [the plans] don't work. They don't change a thing." He eschews being considered excessively cynical but comments that "the nice thing about being in the compensation consulting business is that what they propose will never work, so they have the chance to be hired and start all over again."

Pfeffer asked us to think back to a decade ago, "when Nordstrom department store was doing so well and was the darling of the retail sector." In those days Nordstrom was outperforming other stores, he says. "And because they paid commissions, other department stores immediately concluded it was the way they paid people that made them successful and so began copying them.

"Well, naturally," says Pfeffer, "the Nordstrom pay plan didn't change a thing for the companies that copied it except create a lot of confusion and make people unhappy. Everyone thought it was the way Nordstrom paid their people, when in fact it was their culture."

Pfeffer cites the current example of the Men's Wearhouse, a U.S. menswear retailer doing very well. "What CEO George Zimmer has been trying to do is transform the company's salespeople from clerks into wardrobe consultants, so that instead of just selling someone a blue blazer, they'll also sell him slacks, a shirt and a tie." According to Pfeffer, the salespeople at the company earn a 3 percent commission on the first five hundred dollars they sell a customer, and 7 percent on everything above that amount.

"Predictably," he says, "because the Men's Wearhouse is currently doing exceedingly well, many competitors have copied their commission program." The reason, he explains, is that "it's something they can grab and implement in five nanoseconds."

Pfeffer wisely predicts, "What they won't copy is the exhaustive training the company offers." He adds, "The Wearhouse company culture is based on trust and respect, and their success is due to a document called 'The Covenant' that exists between the company and its salespeople. To imitate that," he says, "would mean real work and would mean working on the creation of a culture."

The words of Nucor's CEO Dan DiMicco ring louder in every chapter: "The culture is the system and the system is the culture."

But the questions remain. How do highly productive companies pay their workers? What's the best way to pay people if you want to improve productivity? How can we prove that *Less Is More?*

It's Not the Money

In companies without a culture, *money* frequently becomes the culture by default. It's everyone for himself . . . the hell with coworkers, the product, the customer or the company.

Based on exhaustive research, Herbert Simon, the noted economist and Nobel laureate, arduously maintained that using market-based systems (such as individual pay for performance) inside an organization would mean you'd no longer have an organization but would instead have created a market.

Dr. Pfeffer sums up Simon's findings by saying, "The essence of organizations is interdependence, and when these interdependent parts are put at war with one another with things like individual pay for performance, the net result is the creation of a completely dysfunctional environment."

By contrast, the highly productive companies we studied largely use *group* productivity-based compensation to drive and constantly reinforce their culture. Initially we considered the possibility that the pay plans of the companies were what steered them toward higher productivity. On closer examination we realized that, instead, their pay plans serve a much bigger goal; they drive and reinforce the culture that in turn increases productivity.

Workers in such companies thrive in their jobs for a number of reasons:

- They're part of group-based work.
- They're not really working but playing a game because everything is scored.
- They're respected and heard by management.
- They feel they're making a difference and that their work matters.

A recent study by William Mercer Consulting replicated what's been proven in hundreds of similar studies: less than 20 percent of workers in companies with low turnover cite compensation as a major concern, while more than 60 percent of workers in high turnover companies name compensation as a primary complaint. When people are happy in their jobs, they aren't apprehensive about money, but when people are unhappy, money concerns reign supreme.

If job satisfaction, not money, is the primary motivator for employees at highly productive companies, then why do these companies bother to use productivity-based compensation plans?

The answer is deceptively simple.

Companies need to pay their workers, so why not help workers feel as if they control their own future and financial destiny? This is the dignified and respectful way—simply another method to drive home the fact that management trusts the employees.

Pay for productivity is also an effective way for companies to identify who will and who will not fit into their culture. Those who simply don't fit at a place like Nucor, SRC, Warehouse and Ryanair will opt out of the system for fear that they won't earn enough to live on. The people who fit and work within the culture will find themselves well rewarded.

The pay-for-productivity plans used by the companies we studied share a number of characteristics. Each plan is:

- Capable of quickly weeding out people who won't fit in
- Organized as group-based

- Built to drive the team spirit
- Designed to provide constant reinforcing of the culture
- Easy to understand
- Financially rewarding for hard and smart work

Weeding People Out

At Nucor everyone works on a team and each week's paycheck reflects how much steel their team produced the preceding week. When DiMicco reports that some of the people the company hires don't fit the Nucor culture and quit, he says it's because they're unable to successfully work on a team. Being paid for what their team produces is precisely what the Nucor culture is all about.

When you spend time in a Nucor plant and talk to the workers, it's almost as if they speak with one voice. They explain how things work: "When we get a new member on our team, they get ninety days to make it."

A worker in a Utah Nucor plant told us that during the ninety days, the new hire is told what to do and how to do it. Everyone pitches in to train them because "they're going to make us all some money. But if at the end of ninety days they're not a team member making us money, they're out of here fast."

Herb and Marion Sandler have been running Golden West Financial/World Savings for forty years and employ almost six thousand people. Yet during that time they've had practically no personnel changes in management. "Once people become part of our family— our culture," Herb says, "they don't leave. In the past twenty-five years we've only lost three executive team members we would have liked to keep." The operative phrase in Sandler's statement is *once they've become part of our culture*"—a culture clearly not for everyone.

"When we acquired World Savings," he says, "one of the managers of the company we purchased came to see me and said, 'I've never seen a company operate like this. It's incredible, but I'm going to leave because it's not for me.'"

Herb explains what was really meant was that World is an incredibly productive company and expects a lot. "We're competitive. We want to win. There's no place here for anyone to goldbrick. And our compensation plans reflect our beliefs and hard-work culture."

Group-based Companies

Some of the world's most productive companies don't offer the best salaries—and they know it. IKEA is a good example. Kent Nordin, the manager of IKEA for Australia, says, "When it comes to compensation, we're not going to be the company that pays the best and we're not going be the one to pay the least. We are going to be somewhere in the middle.

"But when you talk to people, you'll learn that's not the reason they work with IKEA." The reason people chose to be at the company has very little to do with the money, he says. "What people like about IKEA is that they have a chance to take on big responsibilities at a very early age."

Nordin claims, "There's no better place than IKEA for someone who is eager to learn and willing to move around. The career path can be very quick, very fast. Many of us in the company have experienced having enormous responsibilities and tasks while we were very young. I was in my twenties and running a huge operation with more than four hundred people in Germany and couldn't even speak the language."

Money never factored into Nordin's decision-making equation because he was happy with his job. IKEA trusted him, gave him projects that mattered and put him to work with a team.

Nordin confesses, "Sometimes it's kind of scary, but it's amazing that most people rise to the occasion and manage quite well. IKEA proves that you can start to give people responsibility very early."

IKEA employees rise to the occasion when challenged (and they're challenged frequently) because they love their jobs. The reward comes when they are promoted at the end of a project, which yields more responsibility and, consequently, more pay.

As mentioned earlier, SRC's Jack Stack is proud of the fact that his company changes bonus programs frequently—more than twenty different ones in the past twenty years—and each is tied to the accomplishment of specific team objectives. "We're constantly looking to the future and asking ourselves where we might become weak. After all, we have people's lives at stake here and they must be protected."

Stack says, "What we try to do with all of our compensation programs is drive out weakness. For example, we might have great revenues in one of our plants but if we learn that a competitor is turning their inventory twenty times and we're turning ours six times, we're eventually going to be in trouble. So we immediately create a team bonus program tied to doubling our inventory turns, and we'll spend an entire year figuring out how to get [there]."

Driving Team Spirit

The husband-and-wife Sandler team concentrates on making World Savings a place that the right team members don't want to leave. Marion Sandler is quick to share her thinking that "people have to have job satisfaction. You can't pay people enough to work in a place they don't enjoy and where they aren't surrounded by other people who share the same kinds of view."

Both Sandlers agree: "You can't build a great company with high turnover. Our goals are very long-term and we look for people who share that value and then compensate them so their long-terms objectives are satisfied, as well as the company's."

A key component of the World Savings salary program is one that is specifically designed to drive the company's culture. The way

World ranks their branches and provides bonuses for their managers and workers is, according to Marion Sandler, key to success. Each branch is ranked on four factors:

1. growth in deposits
2. staying within the agreed operating budget
3. results of branch audits
4. customer service

Three of the criteria are purely quantitative and easy to measure. For the fourth, the company employs mystery shoppers to evaluate each branch's customer service. "We employ people from outside the area to shop our branches. We prefer using our own staff and managers. So, for example, when someone who manages a branch in Colorado spends time shopping California locations, they're not only evaluating but learning as well."

Reinforcing the Culture

In 2001, Michael O'Leary, the CEO of Ryanair, was named by *Fortune* magazine as its first "European Businessman of the Year." During a wide-ranging interview with *Fortune*'s Richard Tomlinson, O'Leary called the people who run British Airways a bunch of "numb-nuts" and referred to the head of another major European carrier as an "incompetent moron."

That kind of abrasive, in-your-face style seems almost like flute music being played by a modern-day pied piper to the 1,700 early-thirtyish types who make up the Ryanair workforce. Whenever O'Leary rails against the government and his competitors, there's a discernible cheer from the company employees, all of whom grew up in the highly regulated economic environments of EU nations. The very spirit of Ryanair is about tweaking tradition and turning conventional wisdom upside down. Therefore it's not surprising that the way the company pays its workforce is vastly different than the compensation schemes at old-line, stuffy European airlines; Ryanair rewards productivity, not tenure or pedigree.

O'Leary is clearly proud that there are no cushy jobs at Ryanair. "Everybody gets paid for what they produce."

Flight attendants at Ryanair, like the steelmakers at Nucor, have lower salaries than those elsewhere in the industry . . . but they know they'll take home more than their counterparts. Their pay is one-third base salary, one-third bonuses from team sales of refreshments and merchandise onboard and one-third bonuses for the number of flight segments they work.

Much of the bottom-line success of Ryanair also results from their high level of aircraft utilization, which comes from establishing a goal of getting each airplane unloaded, cleaned and boarded again within twenty-five minutes. Bonus money goes into a pool each time crews successfully meet this goal. But money is *subtracted* for each failure to meet the goal. You can well imagine that Ryanair team members don't put up with slackers.

The same holds true for cockpit crews, who receive productivity bonuses based on segments flown and for on-time arrivals and departures. The company is quick to point out that all bonus dollars are paid for productivity. Scoring systems and team pay for productivity schemes extend to every area and function of the company excluding aircraft safety.

Easy to Understand

As I travel the world on consulting assignments, giving speeches and doing book research, I frequently have the opportunity to ask many people about what they do, their industries, the challenges they're facing and their points of view.

One of the questions I find myself asking is, "How does your company use compensation to drive productivity?" What I've discovered is that (with the exception of salespeople, who are always able to explain their commission structure because that's how they're paid), there seems to be a surprising disconnect between how top executives and everyone else in a company answer that question. Most CEOs and high-ranking executives seem prepared to explain the way they believe their compensation programs drive and reward productivity. But most workers don't see any connection between how they're paid and the goal of increasing productivity; either they don't even know the company is striving to connect pay with productivity, or they know the company claims there's a connection but think the claim is bull-cocky.

Yet at highly productive companies, everyone clearly understands the connection between working harder, doing it smarter, producing more and their next paycheck.

Rewarding Smart Work

The late Earl Nightingale, known for his success at motivating workforces, once said, "Luck is when preparedness meets opportunity."

Most industrialized nations have a heritage of unionization and may remember how union bosses became an enemy of productivity by telling the rank and file to give only what the company was paying for and "not a moment more." In those days of lunch boxes and strikes, workers seem to have largely followed that lead; if the official start time was nine A.M., there was a mad rush in the doors at one minute before nine. It's a no-brainer that any workforce will be more productive if minds are in gear and engaged when the machines—whether lathes or computers—are started.

So we were both surprised and delighted to find workers of high productivity companies in factories, retail enterprises and service businesses showing up for work early and finishing according to their personal drive and company loyalty. In fact, in the typical Nucor plant, steelworkers regularly arrive as much as an hour before work to "get ready." When asked what they're getting ready for, they explain that when their shift begins, they want to start production immediately and not waste time figuring out what they'll be doing that day. The response would shock many who remember the painful days of steel fences and strike breakers. A refrain that constantly echoed in reply to our question was, "We're here to make some steel and make some money, not waste time."

Consider the competitive advantage that would accrue to any company whose workers took it upon themselves to show up thirty minutes to an hour early just to be prepared to begin working the moment they were able.

Our conclusion: Productivity is not just about payroll; rewarding people is part of a respectful culture.

Ask yourself if you respect your people enough to build into the company culture a direct relationship between how much workers produce or how effectively they perform, and what they're paid. When workers are provided the proper tools, work on teams, are tracked by accurately kept scores and are placed with dignity in control of their own financial destinies—your company productivity will skyrocket. To believe anything else is to believe the worst about people instead of the best.

The next subject for scrutiny is the role of technology in making a business more productive and allowing companies to do more with less. What we found may surprise you.

DIGITIZE

12

The Plug-in Myth

A complex system that does not work is invariably found to have evolved from a simpler system that worked just fine.

—Murphy's Law of Computing

Although I've always prided myself on staying ahead of the high-tech curve, something happened a couple of years ago that really drove home the promise of technology.

I was doing research and wanted to interview a Midwestern U.S. senator. We'd been friends when I was involved in managing the advertising of his earlier congressional campaigns, but we hadn't spoken for a decade. I called his office, explained who I was and left a message. As you might guess, I didn't get a return call. A few days and several follow-up calls later, the breathless and self-important intern answering the phones explained that the senator had many "old friends" and she couldn't possibly relay another message like mine.

"The senator is a very busy man," she lectured. "All I can do is give your message to the assistant to the assistant of the senator's administrative assistant."

I wanted to ask her if she'd like to join me for tea with the Mad Hatter but resisted, fearful she'd put my name on the office nutcase list.

Out of frustration, I entered the senator's first and last name into the people search space on my homepage. Darn. There weren't any matches.

But there was a tempting flashing button that promised to find anybody . . . for a few bucks.

I thought, *What the heck—give it a whirl.*

So I entered his name, typed in my credit card information and e-mail address, clicked submit and went back to work without giving it any more thought.

Less than ten minutes later I heard the sometimes annoying *bee-boom* signaling I had e-mail. The search company had responded much more quickly than I had expected. *Must have failed,* I thought. I opened the message and couldn't believe my eyes.

Staring back at me was a virtual treasure trove of information: the senator's office address and phones, home address and phones in a D.C. suburb, home address and phones back in his home state and even the address and telephone number of what I remembered as his summer home in the northern part of the state. There were even a few hyperlinks to county registrars' offices. With a few dozen clicks and in less than fifteen minutes, I'd bagged his social security number (quite accidentally), and the names of his mortgage lender, insurance broker and kids.

Most people are aghast when I tell this story. Most still don't comprehend how much private information is easily available on the Internet about everyone and for everyone.

I, on the other hand, love it. Technology is fantastic. Consider the following:

The same information that I was able to gather has always been available to a select few. In the past if someone had the inclination to know something and had the resources (meaning the money), he or she could readily gather the same information. All it took were footwork and time. The people able to collect such information were afforded a distinct advantage. Knowledge was power, yes, but it was power based on money.

Now, instead of footwork and dollars, it's keystrokes and know-how; it's fast and it's either free or costs pennies. Any computer-savvy teenager with a modem has access to the same information as a titan of industry. The same information is available to everyone. Technology represents the democratization of everything.

Neither Knowledge nor Technology Creates a Competitive Advantage

In this current climate, where does competitive advantage lie? Not in knowledge. Not any longer. No, today's competitive advantage lies in *the ability to execute*. (If you want a glimpse of what our lives will be like in the not-too-distant future, read my friend Ray Kurzweil's *The Age of Spiritual Machines*. It's an accurate, nail-biting, page-turner that will convince you that a future that seems far away is actually very close.)

Technology will continue to dramatically impact and alter the lives of everyone on the planet; that's the good news. The bad news, for anyone waiting for the technology fairy to wave a magic wand over his business and make it magically more productive, is wrapped up in a single word of the preceding sentence: *everyone*.

If you happen to be a systems or software salesperson or engineer, you might be reading this book while on an airplane. I suggest you stop chewing your peanuts before you read the next few paragraphs; otherwise you might choke.

Nothing counts, tracks, predicts and follows stuff better than technology, and eventually improvement in any of those areas theoretically reduces costs and results in improved productivity. But unless the software is proprietary—only one company has it—the same benefits can be achieved by every competitor; consequently, no one company can use the technology to achieve decided competitive advantage.

Digitization Doesn't Create a Competitive Advantage

Paralleling our research was a year-long study of productivity conducted by a dozen McKinsey & Company Global Institute staffers. Their findings about information technology mirror ours. In the summary of their study, they point out one of the big fallacies of the fuzzy dotcom thinking that caused so many people to believe the laws of gravity no longer applied—at least not to them.

The McKinsey report demonstrates that between 1995 and 2000, productivity in the United States grew at a stunning 2.5 percent annual rate compared to 1.4 percent annually between 1972 and 1995. Between 1995 and 2000, U.S. companies also happened to double their investment in information technology. Predictably, every fresh-faced new world pundit took to the airwaves and to the printed page and erroneously connected the two facts.

Forecasting a brand-new world, they alleged that because businesses spent nearly $400 billion on technology, productivity increased. "And there's no end in sight," they promised, "as long as companies keep investing in technology." Unfortunately, their soaring promises crashed along with the rest of the dotcom rocket ships.

The McKinsey report debunks the productivity/IT connection, concluding instead that managerial innovation plus new products and services in a few very highly competitive industries accounted for nearly all the productivity gains. In fact, the report points out that in some industries, there was actually a decline in productivity.

Like McKinsey & Company, and much to its disappointment, my research team found that technology hasn't played a pivotal role in allowing the companies we studied to become productivity machines. And in fact there's a double whammy here: some leaders of highly productive companies believe that technology can actually slow companies down and render them *less* productive.

Thinking back to 1992, Pat Lancaster says, "Before we began using *kaizen* to become productive, we were actually one of IBM's dar-lings—a platinum-level customer using every machine and program they could sell us.

"You should have seen our factory back then." He remembers the nightmare of having racks of the wrong parts stacked to the rafters. Some were so old they had collected a thick layer of grime and gray dust.

"The promise of technology," says Lancaster, "was that this huge mainframe computer would run a materials requirements planning program and order the goods for whatever we were manufacturing. The theory was that technology would allow us to synchronize peo-ple's tasks, the arrival of parts and the needed assembly materials at just the moment we needed them and we'd be a lot more produc-tive." Lancaster says, "Besides the requisite software glitches that al-ways occur, there are a couple of realities you need to take into consideration when you expect technology to make you more pro-ductive."

Most technology assumes a perfect world—that suppliers will have delivered every component needed for assembly so that every-thing will be on hand. Lancaster warns, "Sometimes that doesn't happen, so you either shut down the line and wait for the parts or build a lot more half-built machines waiting for parts."

So what do you do when a customer wants or needs a product faster than the technology allows? Sooner or later, this always hap-pens and then, according to Lancaster, people start fooling with the system. "The net effect is you end up losing all the value of MRP," be-cause, he explains, "except for the coneheads who run it, nobody else understands how bad they're screwing it up.

"We were trying to be productive and build ten machines at a time," says Lancaster, "and what we had was a nightmare. We'd go to build ten machines and because parts were missing, we'd start an-other ten and get stopped again when more parts were missing." It got so bad that they ended up with more expeditors working on the floor than assemblers.

Ed Constantine and Bruce Thompson of Simpler Consulting make a rapier-sharp point when they say, "One of the bad things about technology is that it brings all the waste along with it. Anytime we encounter people implementing technology without first getting the waste out of the process, they inevitably end up with huge problems."

A business has an obligation to select the right tool to get the job done, Constantine insists, and adds, "Sometimes that right tool involves technology—but not before you've eliminated the waste."

To illustrate his point, he relates the story of one recent quest for productivity. "We had a furniture manufacturer," says Constantine, "with a half-million-dollar computer numerical control machine whose purpose was to cut holes in upholstery. The company had nothing but constant trouble trying to keep this high-tech marvel working."

After evaluating the operation, Ed and his partner realized that all the patterns the company needed could be achieved by a much simpler solution. The company was able to replace the sophisticated half-million-dollar machine with three small tables with spindles on them that cost less than $5,000 each. "In the process, they increased productivity fifty-six percent.

"When we were finished, the simplicity was just unbelievable, breakdowns didn't exist and the training curve was minutes instead of weeks." And "the flow was fantastic."

Technology for Technology's Sake Is Waste

There's no denying that technology has helped all the companies we covered become faster, more nimble and, yes, more productive. For example, Yellow Corp. was able to achieve a 10 percent cost reduction in material procurement through the Internet and a 15 percent cost reduction in customer management because of their Web site. All the other companies have achieved similar kinds of savings. But again, that's the rub. The *same savings*—hence the same increases in productivity are available to all companies. What we didn't find at highly productive companies was the tendency to embrace technology for technology's sake.

In Herb Sandler's opinion, "More money than you can imagine has been wasted down a technology rat-hole by companies playing a game of 'keep up with the Joneses.'" This World Savings guru was not just talking about dotcomers but brick-and-mortar companies doing the technology shag just because everyone else was.

Even though World Savings now boasts a modern and sophisticated 1,700-person workforce at its 500,000-square-foot technology campus in Texas to perform back-office functions, Marion Sandler says, "I remember when we hired someone to head our data processing area and they came in and announced, 'This thing is held together with rubber bands and chewing gum.' He couldn't understand how we were able to provide the level of high-touch customer service we did without having a fancy IT infrastructure at the time."

Herb smiles as he reviews in his mind the sales tactics companies use when trying to convince you that your company is falling behind technologically. "For example, IBM and all the other big hardware or software companies would call and want us to come in and see their latest technology. One of the tactics they used," he says, "was never to let you sit next to another customer. They'd sit us down with one of their people between us and do the hustle with all the latest bells and whistles."

But, he says, "When we analyzed what they were selling, we could see what it would cost us but we couldn't see where the payback was coming from."

Recall that World Savings was the last major financial institution to buy and install ATMs because it recognized that the savings and time-deposit customers who were its primary market didn't have much need for the machines. "It was lovely technology but we just didn't understand how we could make money with them, and we didn't buy the argument that we had to have them because everybody else did." Only in the late nineties, when World made an aggressive move for high-balance checking account customers, did it finally decide to install ATMs.

On the subject of technology Herb Sandler says, "Cost control and productivity come from corporate culture, focus, discipline, the day-to-day grubby work of blocking and tackling, not from computers."

The Great Digital Divider

Two decades ago, soon after I'd started my consulting firm, I decided we needed to produce large amounts of personalized letters and envelopes—a routine task now but back then it was one that required the latest IBM technology. Before long I was the proud owner of an IBM System /6. The darn thing was as big as a small house, required its own special air-conditioned room and operator, but managed (when it wasn't broken down or the operator wasn't away for training) to spit out direct mail at a prodigious rate.

People flocked from all over to witness my new whizbang technology and I enjoyed it so much I promptly purchased four more of the buggers after convincing myself there was a potential profit center in doing personalized direct mail for other companies. (I didn't ask WTGBRFDT and didn't pause to wonder what the connection was between a direct-mail operation and a consulting company. I'm now convinced I was deluded by the desire for more praise from the IBM team and everyone who came to look at my fancy machines.)

One day my assistant called me and said I had an unannounced visitor.

"Who is it?" I asked.

"Just come out here this minute," she insisted. "There's someone here to see the machines." She added, "You'll love it. Get out here, right now. He doesn't have all day."

My curiosity piqued, I responded and found this bearded, chubby guy dressed in khaki fatigues standing in front of the reception desk.

"Mister Jennings," she beamed, "this is Francis Ford Coppola and he's here to see your machines."

Given his appearance, I wouldn't have put a dime in his tin cup if I'd bumped into him begging on the street but I sure knew the name. *How cool*, I remember thinking, *the director of* The Godfather *is here to meet me and see my machines.*

For the next two hours my new "friend" Francis and I hung out together in the glass-walled fishbowl that served as the official System/6 center and talked about the finer points of technology while the firm's one hundred staffers all suddenly found an urgent reason to walk by, pause, look in and do everything but press their noses to the glass walls while still trying to be nonchalant.

It's a good thing the salespeople didn't try to sell me more machines that day. I'd have bought their entire inventory. Francis Ford Coppola was my new buddy and IBM had made it possible.

The story turned out to have an unfortunate ending.

Just a few months later the System/6 machines sat idle. Rival firms had introduced far cheaper and faster technology, I'd fired the temperamental programmer whose tantrums had caused the department to unravel and IBM refused to take back their machines. I hadn't even collected Coppola's autograph so I'd have something to show for my folly and it took me years to pay for the behemoths. Sadly, once he'd purchased his own System/6, my new friend Francis didn't call again.

I'd been victimized by the ego gratification that comes from being admired as an early adopter. I had purchased technology far beyond my current or future needs, thought it would run itself, failed to consider what a diversion it could become and allowed the salespeople to play me like a banjo. The irony is that the entire technology adventure got started because we wanted some letters personalized. Somehow that simple aim was lost.

We'd all have cushy jobs if the answer to every business problem and dilemma came in a small gift-wrapped box containing the latest digital solutions.

When it comes to technology there are several distinct groups of businesspeople. There are those who naively believe in a magical technological solution for leading their business to increased productivity. They're quickly placed on an IT company's sucker list that's labeled, "They'll buy anything."

Then there are those who are genuinely interested in doing the right thing. But some of these have unwittingly surrounded themselves with IT hotshots who are interested in having the opportunity to play with the latest technology and brag to their friends about how IT-cool they are. These brilliant nerds would willingly bankrupt their company in order to have the latest, greatest, best and most cutting-edge technology.

Finally, there are the businesspeople like the ones profiled in this book who are prepared to embrace and invest in technology as a tool when they understand exactly how they'll be repaid in lower costs and/or increased productivity.

Stephen Tindall's The Warehouse didn't hesitate to invest in a radio frequency scanning system for one of its huge distribution centers, fifteen football fields in size. When he realized they'd be able to receive a pallet from a manufacturer, scan it and move it onto one of their dispatch trucks in as little as eight minutes, Tindall was ready to move ahead. The scanning system he finally decided on increased productivity more than 15 percent and paid for itself within two years. But first he asked "WTGBRFDT?"

In the late nineties most steel companies were busy pouring tens of millions of dollars into the technology that would allow them to move online with their sales operations, called "trading" in the steel industry. "E-trading is the future," they argued, and then plunged ahead with such huge investments that they desperately needed to make their forecasts come true. Nucor on the other hand refused to join the mad rush online; Dan DiMicco reasoned that "We don't believe in putting anyone between our customers and us."

While other steel manufacturers were spending their resources on e-trading protocol and Web sites, Nucor decided to invest $100 million dollars in a plant in Indiana that would feature new technology designed to produce steel by casting the molten metal directly into very thin strips. Alan Cramb, codirector of the Center for Iron and Steelmaking Research at Carnegie Mellon University, termed Nucor's work "the greatest technical development in the steel industry in thirty years."

What kind of a financial return will Nucor realize on its technology investments? Let's do the math together. Rejects of "scaled" or damaged steel were running 2½ percent of sheet sales and were costing Nucor $50 million annually. If its new technology reduces rejects by only half, it will pay for the new plant in just four years. These are significant increases in productivity—an ROI that convincingly supports the technology decision.

Visit the Web site of any major airline and then compare it to Ryanair.com. You'll see a dramatic difference in the way Ryanair uses technology versus its money-losing rivals. Nearly 90 percent of all tickets on the airline are booked on its Web site, which is designed to be as simple and utilitarian as the airline itself. The homepage lists all airports served and the lowest airfare for each segment. With a single click a passenger can buy a one-way ticket to any Ryanair destination and repeat the process for a round trip. The only other buttons are for renting a car, purchasing insurance or booking a hotel.

The boldest type on the site lists the airline's punctuality and on-time arrivals for the previous week (generally averaging an enviable 98 percent). The site is simple and clean and has never been down.

The Ryanair site provides a stark contrast to the sites of major carriers that win design accolades and praise from other Web designers but are often complicated and user-unfriendly; many make it seem that the airline is more interested in mining data than in actually selling tickets.

Flow First—Then Digitize

We found that companies that consistently demonstrate the *Less Is More* principle have ruthless and strict criteria for evaluating technological initiatives.

- **Define and map the current flow.**

  Whether it's selling airplane tickets, lending mortgage money or making bagels, there's no way to eliminate waste, cut costs or improve productivity without first knowing exactly the way the process currently happens.

- **Determine the real objective.**

  What's the desired outcome? Is it to decrease costs, increase productivity or improve customer service? Highly productive companies involve the people who perform the actual work in defining their objectives, and then make sure the objectives are quantified.

- **Evaluate the hard costs of developing proprietary versus off-the-shelf solutions.**

  Any technology that you develop and own will give you a brief competitive advantage until it's replicated by another company. If it's proprietary, guard it zealously and fly low.

■ Arduously scrutinize and consider every possible soft cost.

What's the cost of initial and ongoing personnel training? When the technology isn't working, will the entire business be down? How will the technology affect ongoing personnel costs? Will it require additional or less square footage? Again, productive businesses involve workers from every level of the organization in determining these costs.

■ Total the hard and soft costs.

If the proposed dollar costs outweigh the advantages gained, it's no deal and back to the drawing board.

■ Decide the length of time required for financial payback.

Highly productive companies want to earn their money back as quickly as possible. As a rule of thumb, unless the technology will pay for itself within two to three years, it probably warrants further intense scrutiny.

■ Demand and negotiate performance guarantees from vendors and suppliers.

Unless they're prepared to warrant that the technology solution under consideration will perform and accomplish exactly as promised, open negotiations with another company.

■ Negotiate by pitting one supplier against another on price, payment and performance guarantees.

In 2002 Ryanair placed an order for one hundred Boeing 737s with options for another fifty. The company had kicked off the purchase process by running ads in aviation magazines announcing a search for secondhand 737s. This predictably brought salespeople from every aircraft manufacturer to Michael O'Leary's

Dublin office. By pitting one manufacturer against another, and with the prospect of the company buying late-model used airplanes instead of new ones, Ryanair was able to eventually snag the deal of the century.

Eventually O'Leary bought his technology—the airplanes—for a reported 50 percent off the list price of $60 million, paid only 15 percent down, and Boeing reportedly had to guarantee the resale value of the planes.

■ Before committing, reevaluate everything one more time, asking WTGBRFDT.

To make absolutely certain there's no ego involved and that a case of "my building's bigger than yours" or "my technology's faster than yours" hasn't bubbled to the surface, and that the real reason behind acquiring the new technology is to improve productivity, ask Marion Sandler's question repeatedly: "What's the good business reason for doing this?"

By our best estimate, the top productive companies in this book have collectively invested more than $20 billion in technology. But each went through a precise decision-making process much like the one listed above, and each plunged in for the right set of reasons.

The bottom-line lesson is that it's people and culture—not technology—that provide productive companies their outstanding competitive advantage.

Arie de Geus spent thirty-eight years with Royal Dutch Shell directing its group planning efforts, is the author of the highly acclaimed *The Living Company* and serves as a visiting fellow at the London Business School. As a result of his vast research into the history of companies he concludes, "If you view companies as a species the average life span of a business is now less than twelve years in developed western nations." How are highly productive companies able to keep everyone on the same page day in and day out for decades without missing a beat? Nucor has an unbroken string of thirty-one years of wins. The Sandlers have been at it for forty years and are still going strong without any plans for slowing down. For IKEA it's more than fifty years of proving its ability to keep its workforce motivated and constantly becoming more productive. Our conclusion is that these companies have managed to survive, thrive and excel because they've been able to keep everyone on the same page. We'll find out how they do it in the next section.

MOTIVATE

13

Keeping Everyone on the Same Productivity Page

Unless a message is consistent with the culture it will be seen as being false.

—Dr. James Campbell Quick

It was the kind of day to encourage dreams of the perfect putt in the hearts of golfers. On such a day a few years ago, a friend of mine who worked in real estate sales called me looking for a partner. He asked if I wanted to play hooky. The eighteen holes were out there just waiting for the two of us. Though I said I couldn't because both cars had been spoken for that day, he was delighted to have found I was both willing and ready to play hooky.

"No problem," he said, relieved to have found a partner in crime, "I'll drive down and pick you up."

Thirty minutes later I stood at the foot of my driveway with my brand new Big Bertha driver safely in hand and my bag of clubs leaning against the stone wall. My fantasy was clear; Big Bertha would help me drive every ball at least three hundred yards straight down the middle of a fairway. (A guy can dream, can't he?) The sound of his Cadillac nudged me back into reality. So I grabbed my bag and shouted at him over the purr of the motor, "My clubs. Pop open the trunk."

As he clicked the electronic opener, he rolled the window down so

I could hear his answer. "You can try but I don't think they'll fit. I've got a lot of stuff back there."

Boy, oh boy, was he right! My clubs would have to go in the backseat. His trunk was jammed with books, audiotapes and videos with cover credits like Zig Ziglar, Tom Hopkins and Wayne Dwyer, and titles like *Go for It, Do It* and *Slam Dunk the Moment*.

I shut the trunk, maneuvered my golf bag onto the backseat, and as we pulled out I asked, "What the heck is all that stuff in the trunk?"

"That's my stash," he said. "The stuff that keeps me going."

I thought, *Here's a guy making a few hundred thousand dollars a year and he needs that stuff to keep him going?* It didn't seem to make sense. I knew my questions might seem intrusive, offensive and off-putting but I just couldn't help myself.

"What do you mean 'keep you going'?"

"I hate my job," he said. "I use the tapes and books to try and stay pumped up."

He hated what he did for a living? How sad.

The items he had in his trunk are all big sellers, so a lot of people must need the same help he had prescribed for himself.

Various trade associations estimate that American companies spend as much as $150 billion annually to motivate their workers. According to one trade association, American businesses spend $25 billion just on travel and small gifts as motivational items.

If these various estimates are even close to being correct, it would mean that on average companies spend more than $1,100 per employee per year (using the U.S. Bureau of Labor Statistics figure of 142 million workers) on hiring speakers, buying books and tapes, running contests and trying almost anything to successfully dangle that carrot at the end of a stick in return for more productivity. Even for a company with a few hundred employees, that's not chump change. And remember, this estimated amount doesn't include cash payments and bonuses for productivity; those are reflected in compensation figures and so are impossible to estimate.

Another Big Surprise

Here comes another big surprise. Are you ready for this?

Highly productive companies don't count on traditional motivational tactics to achieve their astonishingly high levels of productivity.

Before we started our research, I guessed this would be the easiest chapter to write—filled with tactical content on how highly productive companies give trips to high producers, cool trinkets for exceeding projections, special parking privileges for producing more than other teams and washtubs filled with money of various denominations where high producers go fishing and grab a fistful of money. (That list was easy for me to write: those are all motivational methods I've used in my businesses. Yep, even the one about fishing for dollars.)

When the research team finally connected the dots, we realized that highly productive enterprises don't rely on traditional motivational methods to become and stay productive. My choice was either to present just that simple, straightforward observation and allow you, the reader, to draw your own conclusion—rendering this a very short chapter—or to dig a little deeper and try to answer the key question: If highly productive companies don't employ the same motivational tactics and programs as most companies, how *do* they motivate their workers?

The simple answer is, "They don't have to." Which clearly requires an explanation.

Motivation Defined and a Startling Truth Explained

Both the dictionary definition of the word "motivate" and its contemporary usage are strikingly close: to cause a person to act in a particular way.

According to the experts, there are two types of motivation: extrinsic and intrinsic. For a layman like me, that means external and internal. A man who helped people understand the difference between the two was the academic and author Dr. James Campbell Quick. He also led us in a direction where we were able to begin differentiating between the use of motivation at highly productive companies and the way it's handled by most business.

Dr. Quick is a retired U.S. Air Force Reserve colonel who was awarded the Legion of Merit. Currently he's the director of the doctoral program in business administration at the University of Texas, and past associate editor of *The Academy of Management Executive*. And with fourteen books on the subject of the workplace, he's a widely acknowledged expert.

"People are born motivated," asserts Dr. Quick. "It's the natural condition. Look at little kids," he says, "and you can easily observe the two basic instinctual drives; one is to feel safe and secure and the other is to explore and master the world.

"The instinctual drive to master the world, which almost everyone has," he says, "is the genesis of our motivation to do things like jump tall buildings and run fast." The big problem occurs "when people find themselves in organizations where their natural energy and drives are frustrated and blocked by a whole variety of bureaucratic mechanisms."

To cut to the chase in explaining the big difference between highly productive and humdrum companies, you may want to read these next words over a few times. We think the following idea from Dr. Quick is among the most important concepts in this book:

"The real challenge is to spend less time trying to design motivational programs and more time figuring how to get out of the way of people trying to do good things."

We believe that the assessment offered by Dr. Quick is correct, which clearly means that companies would fare better to stop investing the $150 billion they presently spend on "motivation" and use that money instead to destroy the bureaucratic mechanisms that prohibit productivity (see Chapter 4).

When we discussed the companies in this book with Dr. Quick and explained what we were finding, he sighed the knowing sigh of an experienced clinical psychologist and said, "The way you're describing what takes place in these companies is that each seems to have created a highly competitive but cooperative system."

If you tick off a mental list of the companies we've researched, Dr. Quick's diagnosis is right on target. While Ryanair, Lantech, The Warehouse Group, IKEA, World Savings, Nucor, Yellow and SRC Holdings are all extraordinarily competitive, their successes rely on cooperative efforts rather than individual achievement.

"When competition within an organization is directed at an external goal or objective, a highly productive cooperative culture can be created. The real danger is when internecine warfare breaks out within the organization. That inevitably results in competition becoming self-destructive, the organization becomes dysfunctional and eventually you see a closing down of the system as people hold back information."

Quick cautions that when that kind of competition occurs, people start behaving in ways they believe are good for themselves and don't care if the results are destructive for the company.

A Stroke of Brilliance from the Irishman

During the course of our research, there was an ever-present albeit unspoken friction between the researchers and me. Even though Ryanair had passed all the tests, the team sometimes wondered if I had made a mistake in allowing a rogue member like CEO Michael O'Leary into the group.

Although no one can deny the stunning financial and productivity performance of Ryanair, the fact is that O'Leary simply didn't seem to fit the profile that emerged of all the other CEOs. By contrast to the humility and understatement of a Stephen Tindall of The Warehouse Group, the matter-of-fact directness of Dan DiMicco at Nucor and the gentle demeanor of the Sandlers at World Savings, O'Leary's style frequently borders on the outrageous.

When O'Leary showed up in a stodgy courtroom accused of not delivering a prize won during a contest run by his airline, he wore jeans and a rugby shirt. He blithely refers to Ireland's transport minister as a "Stalinist," and said the group that manages Dublin's airport has a tourist policy modeled after the one in Castro's Cuba. When O'Leary's airline began flying their first route into Germany, he flippantly minimized Lufthansa, that nation's flag carrier, bragging that his airline would be bigger in just a few years. This is a man who routinely mimics complaining customers in a squeaky falsetto voice. Definitely not your typical company chief executive.

As I've mentioned earlier, following the terrorist attacks of September 11, O'Leary accused other airlines of trying to "screw money" out of their governments and urged them to put away their "begging bowls" and cut fares rather than request government assistance. And for many months a picture hung on a wall in the lobby of Ryanair of O'Leary swinging a baseball bat, with the caption "Michael Preparing for His Next Meeting with the Air Regulators."

O'Leary set up all the other big state-owned, subsidized or supported airlines and the anticompetitive regulatory authorities in Europe as the archenemies of the common man. By doing that he provided his workers all the external motivation required to focus them on the task of becoming Europe's biggest carrier. And when O'Leary responds to the question of the future of Ryanair and answers, "World domination, of course," you gain another level of understanding of the motivational brilliance he practices like a religion. He is always searching for the next mountain to climb and in this way keeps his people rallied and on the same page. These are people too busy fighting a common enemy to become distracted. There is no time for internal politics or small human-sized matters. Adventuring with O'Leary bounces these people out of bed every morning.

O'Leary's promise to his workers echoes the lessons of other great and productive companies. He says, "Join us in fighting the good fight against the dark forces, work hard and we won't have layoffs or cut wages." His promise of no layoffs or pay cuts fulfills a universal instinctual need—the need to feel safe and secure. Another basic drive shared by many people—to master their universe and jump tall buildings—is fulfilled by chasing a big objective and being allied against a common enemy.

"Us" Against the World

All the companies we studied have employed the O'Leary principles—albeit less flamboyantly—in order to achieve high productivity. First, they created a safe and secure environment and then they unleashed their forces against a common external enemy or objective.

At Yellow Corp., Bill Zollars used the analysts who predicted the company would be dead within a few years as the target. It was Yellow against the analysts.

Jack Stack, CEO of SRC, used his firm's upside-down 89 to 1 debt to equity ratio and the way a prospective purchaser would value the company as the centerpiece of his rallying effort to have everyone band together and ensure themselves financial security and a future. It was the workers against the world.

At The Warehouse, Stephen Tindall invited his workers to join him in a new egalitarian culture that would pillory the middlemen, importers and government regulators who he believed had been financially victimizing consumers for years. Everyone joining The Warehouse Group became a deputy to a modern-day Robin Hood.

When Ken Iverson promised the employees that Nucor wouldn't lay off workers and that the company would be run in a truly egalitarian manner, he set up all the other steel manufacturers as the bad guys without precisely saying so. His workers intuitively understood they had to really produce and make the culture work in order for their safe and nurturing environment to continue. It was Nucor against the way things had always been done.

When his company's prized patents expired, Pat Lancaster realized it would have to dramatically alter the way it produced and delivered goods or eventually perish. Pat used "waste" as the unifying external objective and his workers attacked it with zealous ardor. It was a fight against extinction.

Ingvar Kamprad of IKEA used the appealing argument of the "haves and the have-nots" to build the planet's only global furniture brand by proclaiming the purpose for his company's existence was to democratize the world and make quality home furnishings available for the nonaffluent. It was and is the noble fight for a better everyday life for the people Kamprad referred to as "the many."

When Herb and Marion Sandler bought World Savings, they used as their motivator the fact that their company would be a true meritocracy. They were able to point to all other banks and savings and loans as good-old-boy environments of privilege that routinely denied admission, membership and positions of responsibility and authority to women. When deregulation took place and their competitors got into trouble by rushing into all kinds of wild lending practices and speculative ancillary businesses, the Sandlers were quick to add the simplicity of their business model to the equation. World Savings became the best place to work. It was a company that took care of and grew its people and wouldn't imperil their collective futures by irresponsible conduct. The big motivator for the workforce at World became the difference between "them" and "us." It was and is a classic fight between the right way and the wrong way.

A business manager who wants to become more productive can ensure having a motivated workforce by using an external motivator to keep the entire organization on the same page.

But before rushing out to select an external motivator like some flavor of the month, the manager, executive or business owner should be cautioned that setting up a straw man to temporarily rouse or enthuse the workforce is *manipulation*, not motivation.

What is truly different about the external motivator used by the brilliant leaders of these best companies is that it truly represents their "view of the world" and is far more than a superficial manipulative tool. It's their life's work, it's authentic and it supports their personal drive to achieve unprecedented productivity.

Former athlete Bill Zollars is a coach-CEO fervently committed to diverse workplaces, to the value of the customer and to defying the naysayers by winning. Jack Stack's eyes become moist when he talks about building companies that provide financial security for his workers. To prove that it's never been about the personal accumulation of money but doing good work, Stephen Tindall has given his wealth to a foundation that provides for the needy, underprivileged and less fortunate.

It's easy to imagine Dan DiMicco, a physically formidable man, marching through a Nucor plant and being capable of pitching in to perform any physical task or challenge that confronts him. But Dan becomes reverentially quiet and humble when discussing the fact that he was selected as guardian and CEO of a company that gives $2,500 annually to the child of every employee attending a community college, vocational institution or university.

When you watch Pat Lancaster hanging out in the factory with workers recalling stories of the old days—how unproductive they'd been but how they fought the fight and won—it's like listening to a group of crusty veterans recounting a monumental victory on the battlefield. Spend time with an employee of World Savings and you quickly realize they believe in the company, their personal security and the direction of the enterprise.

The highly productive companies we studied are all strikingly similar to what Dr. James Campbell Quick described as a model for study: the military.

"Most military systems," he says, "are good examples of open, healthy, collaborative systems where people are acting not only in their best interests but in the collective best interests of everybody else.

"The military," he asserts, "is a place where members stand up for the greater good. They're not serving just for personal gain but are in it for the collective sense of well-being." Not everyone would agree with his sense of how the military operates, but in Dr. Quick's view, "Great military organizations can be characterized as having environments with no holds barred, everything on the table, frank discussions. An environment where followers are allowed to challenge leaders and superiors in respectful ways with honest information."

Just as the military wouldn't try to boost productivity by offering a free trip to Hawaii for the infantryman who killed the greatest number of enemy soldiers or used the fewest bullets, the companies profiled in this book don't employ short-term manipulative bribes to achieve their high levels of productivity.

Manipulation or Motivation

Any business that finds it must constantly resort to a parade of contests, hype and rewards to keep the workplace productive is manipulating their people rather than truly motivating them. This is a company that will eventually prove for itself its self-fulfilling prophecy that it can't trust its workers.

Unless an increased level of productivity is maintained after a contest, promotion or special initiative has run its course, chances are the action wasn't motivational but manipulative. While there are very few statements able to win near universal agreement, here's one almost everyone will agree on: "People don't like being manipulated." If they can't find a better place to be, workers might put up with some manipulative tactics in the short term. But the moment someone can get away from a manipulative environment, they'll be out the door.

Back in 1912, Frederick Taylor, the father of scientific management, said in testimony before the U.S. Congress, "We can argue about productivity standards all day long but what really needs to happen is to get management and labor working together. When that happens, an enterprise will collectively move forward and the financial results will be naturally achieved. The danger," he said, "is when the financial objectives of an organization are placed in front of its mission or purpose." Taylor's conclusion was that financial performance is the *consequence* of business and must never become the driving force.

When managers encourage a financial objective as the sole reason for the business's existence, they will ultimately be forced to manipulate the workforce to achieve this goal. Management can wear blinders and call it motivation; I say if it walks like a duck and quacks like a duck, it's probably a duck.

Authentic Motivation

We found three steps used in common by the companies we studied to permanently motivate their workforces, and they make a prescription for other companies:

1. Create a safe and secure workplace.

Create a workplace where workers aren't under constant threat of layoffs. Also beware of the siege mentality: workers know when the leadership is ceding control of the organization to lenders and stock market analysts, and fear seeps in.

Highly productive companies take the following steps to create safe and secure environments.

Give meaning to work. The world's most productive companies institutionalize motivation by taking their employees' sense of well-being and happiness into account by giving them meaningful work.

Alfie Kohn, author of *Punished by Rewards,* advises that people must be able to see a connection between what they're doing and the overall goals of the organization. "If you're giving people deadly, dull, pointless tasks to do, then don't be surprised if there may be a few members of our species who would not be intrinsically motivated to do what you're asking them to do."

Some consider Kohn a radical thinker but he does make a sharp point. Who wants to show up every day to a job where you don't feel as if you're contributing anything to some greater good? It's up to the supervisor, leader or manager to help workers make that connection every single day.

Lars-Goran Petersson, in charge of purchasing coordination for IKEA, told us that founder Ingvar Kamprad always said that "the job must be more than just the hours between morning and evening to make some money for rent and food. A job is such a big part of a person's life that it must be something they enjoy."

Make workers stakeholders and give them responsibility. In studying these companies, we found that a big part of that feeling of "meaning" comes from the employees' personal stake in their work. These companies prove the proposition that when people are given responsibility, most will step up to the plate. That's in contrast to many companies where managers breathe down people's necks, micromanage and then struggle with the consequence of their people not performing well.

At SRC, employees are given autonomy to innovate on the job. Jack Stack says, "The problem we have in the U.S. is that we teach people how to become automatons. We do not teach innovation." He adds, "Most employees aren't allowed to think on the job. They are simply asked to complete a task, often the same task over and over again, and given no responsibility for the process."

So Stack begins by teaching his employees business fundamentals, and, when he's comfortable with their basic working knowledge, he lets them loose to think and act; his results have been phenomenal. "Once you understand that you've got to do something about your weaknesses," he says, "then innovation takes over." When employees are the stakeholders, they take it upon themselves to innovate and improve the process.

He proclaims that his system gives his employees "psychic ownership," which he explains this way: "The salespeople own the sales line, and the discount line, the allowance line, and the receivable line." Relate business back to the fundamentals of a balance sheet, he says, and all of a sudden you realize that "the income statement is nothing more than people, and that someone is responsible for each one of those lines."

The same holds true at IKEA, Lars-Goran Petersson told us. "We've found that if you give people responsibility, they take it. IKEA is a company made up of people taking initiative and not about managers pointing at people and telling them what to do. The culture is based on providing workers the freedom to do their job and it is of course expected they'll do it."

When everyone is made a stakeholder and there are clear responsibilities for each function, the employees working in those functions are happier and naturally become more productive because *they* are in charge. It becomes *their* line, *their* department, *their* bagel shop.

Allow mistakes. At IKEA, employees are given high levels of responsibility at an early stage in their tenure. As you've read in a previous chapter, it's not unheard of for employees in their mid-twenties to manage a store with many hundreds of employees and tens of millions of dollars in revenue. How does IKEA ensure that inexperienced employees won't make horrible mistakes? The answer is simple: they don't.

In fact, they encourage their employees to make mistakes. Ingvar Kamprad writes in *A Furniture Dealer's Testament,* "Our objectives require us to constantly practice making decisions and taking responsibility, to constantly overcome our fear of making mistakes. Only while sleeping one makes no mistakes. Making mistakes is the privilege of the active—of those who can correct their mistakes and put them right."

Yellow's Greg Reid often talks about CEO Bill Zollars's acceptance of people who make mistakes. "It shows that you're trying," proclaims Reid, who admits to having made many mistakes himself. "Bill expects us to make mistakes," he adds. "It's the only way to learn how to not make more mistakes."

Foster teamwork. Yellow's Bill Zollars says that when he arrived at Yellow in the mid-1990s, "There was no teamwork, there was only an impenetrable silence between the functions. The people in sales didn't talk to the people in operations and the operations people wouldn't talk to finance. It was endemic throughout the company."

Zollars set up an enemy—the people forecasting the demise of Yellow—and began uniting the workforce. Having an enemy makes employees feel they are part of the team trying to defeat an opponent.

Encourage diversity. Another surprise that awaited Zollars upon his arrival at Yellow was how uniform his management team was. "The lack of diversity in the company was scary," he admits. "The first meeting I had with the corporate officers, there were twenty-one white guys sitting in a row and they had all been only in the trucking industry their entire career. There wasn't anybody in the room that had been in another industry." As if this wasn't bad enough, he later realized that most of them hadn't even worked for any other company. "Not only was there no ethnic diversity but there was no cultural diversity of experience in the room, which was also very frightening," he says. Zollars credits much of Yellow's success and productivity to the company's newly diverse workforce. Highly productive companies thrive on the different opinions and viewpoints that new employees from other cultures and foreign industries bring. They can often immediately spot problems and devise creative solutions because they're unfamiliar with the status quo and have no need to defend it.

Note: As a counter to the argument that "the same rules don't apply for publicly traded companies" because they have to answer on a quarterly basis to Wall Street, we'd point out that Yellow, World Savings, Ryanair, Nucor and The Warehouse Group are all publicly traded firms. We can only imagine with a bemused smile the reactions of Dan DiMicco, Stephen Tindall, Bill Zollars and the Sandlers if an analyst told them how to run their businesses. O'Leary would pick up his bat and say something that would have to be bleeped. Successful executives manage their business, not their share price.

2. Find an external enemy to fight.

Probably not waste, analysts or airport regulators, but something tailored to the situation of your own organization. Direct your company's competitive spirit at a significant external goal. Keep everyone focused on achievement rather than engaging in competition against each other.

3. Then get out of the way.

Because they trust that their group of carefully selected people will do the right things, successful executives get out of the way and let them at it.

Whoa—Wait a Minute

Observant readers may believe they've just uncovered a classic case of "Do as I say, not as I do."

After all, in previous chapters we've laid out how World Savings regularly ranks its branches and pays bonuses to the winning teams for increased deposits, favorable audits and customer satisfaction, how SRC frequently changes bonus plans based on vulnerabilities it's endeavoring to eliminate and how teams of flight attendants for Ryanair receive commissions and bonuses for selling food, beverages and merchandise onboard.

As a reader who has stuck with me this far, you've earned the right to ask, "If those are not pay for play, and classic examples of the same motivational tactics that you have dissed as manipulation in this chapter, then what are?"

The difference between the way the companies profiled here employ motivational tactics and the way many other businesses use them is that highly productive organizations only employ tactics that will help them successfully drive their cultures in the *long term*.

Less successful businesses will engage almost any tactic that has the promise of an immediate payback, with complete disregard for the long term, believing—if they think about it at all—that any negative impact will occur on another person's watch.

In unproductive companies, a ragtag collection of tactics frequently becomes the culture. In productive companies, the tactics drive the culture.

A Story About Motivation

I believe a recent personal experience serves to drive home an important point about the differences in the role of motivation at highly productive and nonproductive companies.

Have you ever experienced a sinking feeling of helplessness and utter despair where the only alternative seemed to be escape?

Not long ago I was invited to give the final wrap-up keynote address for a company holding a two-day retreat for several hundred of its key salespeople and managers. My practice is to ask the person hiring me if I'm allowed to show up early in the day to get a feel for the group, meet some of the people and gather a sense of the audience's mood. Unless highly confidential and proprietary information is being presented, they almost always say yes.

In the case of this particular CEO, his response was an enthusiastic "No problem, we'd love to have you."

So, scheduled to speak in late afternoon, I showed up shortly after the lunch break, seated myself discreetly in the back of the darkened auditorium and prepared to soak it all in. Even though the company does business in the embattled telecommunications business where almost every company started taking tough body blows in the year 2001, I wasn't prepared for what I was about to witness.

The afternoon began with a hostile presentation from a sales manager who played to two audiences—one threatening message intended for the group in the room, and a distinctly different message for the CEO sitting in the front row. After each threat and exhortation to do better that he delivered to the employees, he'd actually look at the CEO like a son trying to impress Dad at a Little League game, wait for a fatherly nod of approval and then continue delivering the next salvo in his hostile assault. He was really beating them up.

Then came the senior VP, who continued in the same bullying and threatening style—announcing plans for layoffs if the group's performance didn't improve, hurling caustic remarks about commission structures and whipping them about how much they made and how easy they'd had it. And threatening that pay plans would quickly change if sales didn't improve fast.

I sank lower and lower in my chair, embarrassed to be there. Why had they hired me and what relevance would my remarks about the world's fastest and most productive companies have on a roomful of wounded sales executives and market development personnel?

Finally the SVP finished his tirade, announced a coffee break and teased the room about my upcoming speech. I wanted to be any other place in the world than there. *Scotty, beam me up,* I silently prayed.

During the break, the top executives huddled around, welcomed me and pumped my hand saying how happy they were I was there. "Well, as you just saw," bragged the CEO, "we tell it like it is in this company. We don't have any secrets and don't pull any punches." And then he added, "Now it's your job to pump them up and get them all excited. Good luck!"

I did the speech, got a standing ovation, signed books and talked with the attendees. Many said things along the lines of "That's the most motivational speech we've ever heard."

Later, as I was struggling to load my bags into a taxi outside the hotel, one of the participants came up, thanked me, shook my hand and offered a thoughtful "I'm sorry you had to see the first part of the afternoon's session. Your message was great and appreciated. It's just too bad this company won't ever do the things you talk about. What's even sadder," he said, "is they're convinced they do." His concluding remark sums up the plight of many: "The problem is that everyone has to have a job, don't they? And this is where I happen to work."

Our research for this book gave convincing evidence that managers of highly productive companies never manipulate their workers or delude themselves. They understand that every message, pay plan, promotion, contest, measurement and program must be consistent with the values, the system and the culture. Short-term manipulative tactics aren't the currency of these companies. They've discovered that *Less Is More* when it comes to motivation.

My final task on this journey is to examine the personality of the leaders of the companies we studied, to determine the traits they share and the principles they hold vital in their leadership of productive organizations. That's where we're headed in the last chapter.

EMBODY

14

A Lean Spirit

Management is doing things right; leadership is doing the right things.
—Peter Drucker

Because I view it as crass commercialism to promote previous books or commercial materials within the text of a new book, I had been determined not to refer to my last work. However, its subject matter relates very closely to the main thrust of this chapter. I hope you'll indulge me this single mention.

It's Not the Big That Eat the Small . . . It's the Fast That Eat the Slow revealed how truly fast companies charge ahead despite the speed bumps that prevent most businesses from thinking fast, deciding fast, getting to market fast and maintaining momentum. One of the discoveries my coauthor and I made was that instead of having traditional "vision" and "mission" statements, fast companies instead all had a cause. Following the book's release we were deluged by companies seeking an answer to the question, "How can we come up with a 'cause' for our company?"

Because "culture" is the dynamic story of the highly productive companies featured in the pages of this book, I'm guessing there's a question that might keep me very busy in the near future: "How do we go about creating a culture that leads to high productivity?" To avoid leaving you wondering, this chapter explains the qualities we found embodied within the cultures of the organizations we included in this book—not what they do (we've already covered that) but why they do what they do, how they make it stick and how other businesses can do the same.

Indeed, some amazing people have led these companies to making their chosen business model perform with the precision of a world-class athlete. No matter how much digging we did for their secrets, we eventually realized there was no magic bullet involved in their success. Peter Drucker would justifiably admire the thinking and follow-through of each of these companies and especially of their leaders.

If there's anything supernatural about these businesses, it's the people who founded, led and in some cases continue to lead them. Because each was or is an inspirational leader, our final study led us to an examination of the cultural traits shared by these people and organizations, and a final big question: "How can a manager embody the traits of extraordinarily productive businesses within their own organizations?"

From the get-go we suspected that the strong personalities of each of the leaders would dominate every aspect of their businesses. But we didn't find that. To the contrary, the more we researched—through virtually every level of the organizations—the more we met people just as capable of speaking to the culture and values as the CEO. That simply doesn't happen in most companies and was one of the most striking findings during the course of our research.

Typically if you ask someone working on a loading dock, call center, assembly line, sales department or retail sales floor to explain the culture of their company, she would stare at you dumbfounded. Finally she might manage a response equivalent to "Sorry, that's not my area. I don't know, I only work here; you'd have to talk to the people in HR or the folks at the head office."

I recall standing in one of The Warehouse stores in Auckland, New Zealand, speaking with a middle-aged associate working the floor. She was able to talk about the company's culture as eloquently as company founder Stephen Tindall. The same thing happened when I made repeated unannounced visits to World Savings branches, made purchases at IKEA, hung with Nucor's steelmakers or flew Ryanair. I remember smiling to myself and wondering if maybe these companies hire only highly articulate people and then run them through an intensive indoctrination program before they meet the public.

The spirit and culture of these companies are as much an intrinsic part of the work environment as lighting or air and therefore are firmly fixed in the minds of everyone who works there. The people know and feel their company culture and so they are able to articulate what they know is true and real.

Not only is measurable productivity a clear result of the culture of a company but in a number of cases the companies we've researched have also proven their cultures to be far more important than even the talented people leading them. Some of these company cultures are withstanding the tests of time and the introduction of new leadership.

A knowledgeable and strong leader initiates a culture and then sweats to make the culture bigger, worthier and more important than any single person—including himself.

Stephen Tindall no longer leads the day-to-day operations of The Warehouse but the company is doing better than ever. Dan DiMicco became the CEO at Nucor but the culture created by Ken Iverson remains firmly in place and the company hasn't missed a beat in growth, productivity or profitability. Ingvar Kamprad has requisitioned himself into a passive role as strategist for IKEA, absent from most of the firm's major decisions, but the company and its culture continue to thrive. Great leaders design and build the cultures that will survive as if the leaders were still running the organization.

Contrast these valid cultures with those of ordinary companies.

Many cultures initiated by less-than-great leaders receive tons of good press but when tested by time or examined by those who understand the signs of strength, they don't pass muster.

The culture of Coca-Cola and the firm's ability to increase earnings every year eventually turned out to be more about squeezing bottlers for money than any set of corporate values. Can anyone forget Ken Lay's smug mug on the covers of *Forbes* and *Fortune* with headlines proclaiming the culture he was building at Enron? Within months of his departure, it imploded. What about Kodak's culture? And journalists couldn't wait to write about the antibureaucratic culture that Percy Barnevik brought to ASEA Brown Broveri (ABB), but later, when orders started tanking and the financial community began raising doubts about the company's ability to pay down bank debt, it turned out that ABB's culture was more about funding Mr. Barnevik's retirement nest egg than about building a real set of shared values.

"Lean" Cultures

"Lean" is a word we use to describe the physical environment, operating model and spirit of highly productive companies.

Recently, you've probably encountered the promise "We're going to become a lean, mean machine" made with gusto by some owner, manager, division head or CEO trying to put the best possible spin on another spate of layoffs or round of cost cutting. Lean has become synonymous with tightening the screws and as such has a generally negative connotation in the minds of the people who work for these new lean, mean machines. (When companies make big pronouncements about suddenly becoming "lean," some interesting questions are raised: Was the enterprise fat before? If so, why and who was responsible? Why don't we start with their heads on a platter first?)

That's not what we mean when we use the word here. In writing of the companies profiled in this book, we use the word "lean" in both a highly complimentary, literal sense and even in a nutritional sense: made up of muscle and no fat.

The Eleven Traits Required for the Leader of a Highly Productive Enterprise

It would take a list of many hundreds of words to accurately portray all the different qualities we found to respect and admire during our interviews with the leaders of our highly productive companies. But eleven traits in particular seemed to stand out—traits we're prepared to defend as being common to each leader. It's a surprising list because some of the words and phrases aren't commonly used in the traditional profiles of leaders and cultures.

These eleven productive traits are—

1. Attention to Detail

Most enterprises would like to proclaim they pay careful attention to detail but they don't. Most are guilty of making decisions on the fly, putting out fires, implementing one initiative after another, being constantly on the prowl for nippy little fixes and doing almost anything to boost profits quickly. So much for attention to detail.

A friend of mine, Mark Glickman, is a CPA in Marin County, California. We were talking one day and he asked about the final list of companies in the book. I began listing them and commenting about the reasons each had been selected. When I named one company— I won't mention the name because I don't want to embarrass Mark— he stopped me to say he knew the CEO of that company from years ago when the company was a client of the large accounting firm Mark was then with. "When they became a client," he told me, "the word went out from the top to everyone in the firm to be on the top of their game because they could *pick fly shit out of pepper*." Responding to my quizzical look, Mark explained, "That's about the highest compliment you can get from a bunch of accountants. It meant nobody should try gleaning over anything because they'd be sure to catch it."

Attention to detail should never be confused with micromanagement. Instead of spending their days poring over reams of reports and numerical analyses, the leaders of the most highly productive companies have each systematically determined the issues that are vitally important for driving their businesses. They spend their time focusing on those issues and delegate watching the back office and operational metrics to trusted people. If one of the important metrics is out of kilter, a savvy executive focuses on it until it's fixed.

One of the reasons for the incredibly high level of productivity at IKEA is that it remains a company committed to following the lessons laid down by its founder, Ingvar Kamprad, who said from the start, "The general who divides his resources will invariably be defeated. IKEA must always be a company that concentrates on one thing at a time. Concentration," he said, "means strength."

2. High Moral Fiber

In response to the question "Would every honest businessperson present please raise your hand?" almost everyone in an audience would lift and salute without a moment's hesitation. But most would also have to fight hard to suppress a nervous giggle because they know the real truth: fibbing, ever-so-slight distortions of the facts, reporting half-truths, exaggerations and promising everything but delivering nothing are routine activities in business. And that's the truth about honesty.

Instead of using the word "honest," Herb Sandler refers to it as "moral fiber," and recounts a significant event that occurred shortly after he and Marion had purchased Golden West.

"In 1966," he says, "the United States faced its first serious liquidity problem since World War Two. And when I say things were tight, I mean there was simply no money in the system.

"Like all other financial institutions," says Sandler, "we had all kinds of loan commitments for money we'd agreed to lend and there was no money to honor our commitments. Savings were going out but there were no new savings coming in. All the other banks and S&Ls were canceling their commitments to borrowers but we made a promise to ourselves to not cancel a single commitment."

Herb remembers with pride that they compiled a list of all the commitments in order of the date they'd been made. "Every day we'd count the dollars coming in from loan repayments, and whenever we had enough, we'd fund another one. Ultimately," he says proudly, "we funded every loan, even though we were losing money. To the best of our knowledge, we were the only company to honor every single commitment."

Marion Sandler finishes Herb's story. "You might wonder why we did that," she asks. "The reason is simple. A great business is built on trust—doing what you promise to do. You can lose your reputation in a single day and you can never get it back. Trust is something you build over your life."

We found the leaders in all the companies we studied were courageously and singularly honest.

3. Embracing Simplicity

While most businesspeople would find the concept of simplicity to be a fascinating subject for a case study, they have come to know that "simple" is anathema to contemporary business. The concept of "simple" has taken on a negative odor of "simplistic"; simple is simply no longer a respected virtue. Except that we found among productive company leaders a keen grasp of the power and meaning of "simple."

In an earlier chapter we discussed how the leaders of highly productive enterprises maintain simple business propositions. In wondering how they've been able to maintain their organization's simplicity—in spite of all the well-intended advice givers who have seductively counseled them to change, modify or expand their model—we think we know how they've been able to resist. These leaders are as lean, uncomplicated and as simple (in the sense of *straightforward*) as the organizations they lead.

When Marion Sandler of World Savings, a woman who can afford any luxury she wants, is asked if she has a chauffeur, she nods and admits that having a chauffeur is her one small indulgence. And then points him out. Her chauffeur is, of course, her husband, Herb, who, she says, although overqualified, does a very reliable job.

In another sign of embracing the value of simplicity, Ingvar Kamprad wonders why companies have large group meetings. "Gathering together hundreds of people," he writes in *A Furniture Dealer's Testament*, "to look at poorly prepared and illegible transparencies is hardly a cost-conscious exercise." He wonders, "Why would a company waste resources on a big, expensive group event when a one-person investigation will usually do just as good a job?"

Once she knew I planned to write about her knitting, Marion Sandler took it upon herself to call me and explain with motherly pride that one of the items she knits every year is a sweater for a holiday arts and crafts benefit the company runs. She sounded like any proud mom whose hand-knit sweater had fetched eight hundred dollars at last year's charitable auction.

From the clothes they wear to their office decor, from the cars they drive to the homes they live in, the leaders in our study are all models of virtue and modesty. Being ostentatious simply doesn't fit the philosophy or the lifestyle of these forthright people.

4. Competitiveness

Most businesses respect and acknowledge, promote and reward, those who can—faster than the other guy—consolidate, acquire and diversify. Today's business environment respects those who are fully prepared to leave concerns about operations, customers, workers and vendors to the person who replaces him after he's been recruited for another, higher-profile position somewhere else.

Jack Stack of SRC sums up the competitive zeal these leaders share and embody when he tells the story of being transferred to Springfield, Missouri, to manage a plant for International Harvester—the company that he and his fellow workers later purchased.

"I came to Springfield," he says, "and I found these salt-of-the-earth Midwesterners who had the greatest entrepreneurial spirit I'd ever encountered. Their attitude was, 'Give us the tools and we'll do the job.' We decided we were going to kick ass and show the world what we could do," he says. "There wasn't a goal we didn't beat. We decided we'd take on every other Harvester factory in the world and win. Here we were," he smiles, "a tiny inconsequential factory taking on the Goliaths and winning."

Stack takes even greater delight as he reaches the story's conclusion. "What we loved the most is the way we pissed off the president of the company because he had to fly here to give us the trophy. He hated it and made his feelings very apparent," Stack says. "And that made us love it even more."

In a typically brash and over-the-top competitive jab at the competition, when Ryanair begins flying into a new country, they've historically named their competition and their intention for war. When they began flying into Belgium, they issued a press release with the headline AU REVOIR SABENA ET L'ARNAQUE (Good-bye Sabena and the rip-off). Predictably Sabena looked to the courts and government authorities for help, while Ryanair looked to the marketplace. Sabena is now out of business.

Slightly more genteel but no less gutsy or competitive is World Savings. Herb Sandler describes himself and his wife, Marion, as being very focused on outcomes in everything they do, not only in business but in all of life. "We have systems here," he says, "but we don't have any time for people to sit around processing stuff. Achieving the desired result is what it's about. We're a competitive company and tell people that unless they share the same outlook, World isn't the place for them."

When asked what she still likes most about the business after al-most forty years, Marion Sandler is quick with her answer. "From a gratification point of view, we're in a wonderful business," she says. "We don't pollute, we enable home ownership to people, many of them minorities, we ethically safeguard people's money. But the other thing that gives us real satisfaction is being highly competitive and outplaying and outwinning the competition."

The leaders of extremely productive companies imbue the organizations they lead with an unparalleled competitive spirit.

5. Long-Term Focus

Long-term focus has become counterintuitive in business. Unless a business hits the quarterly numbers expected by bankers, analysts and Wall Street, the person running the enterprise may be extended one additional quarter to fix things before the tom-tom drums start sounding a warlike tempo to signal a change in leadership.

Nucor's Dan DiMicco says that almost every decision made in business will be different when you have a long-term rather than short-term focus. "The steel business is an extremely cyclical one," he says. "And when times get bad and demand disappears, things can get very tough."

Besides being cyclical, the steel business is also an extremely high asset, capital-intensive business. Nucor's objective is to always be the low-cost supplier, allowing them to sell at lower prices when demand falls. According to DiMicco, "There's no way the company could prosper as it does without sharing a long-term focus with employees, suppliers and customers."

So, as previously discussed, during periods of slow demand—and 2001 was one of those years—the company keeps everyone on the payroll producing what steel they're able to sell, paying people for training, plant refurbishment and getting ready to rock and roll when demand returns.

Even though they led and managed to profitability during 2001, DiMicco and all the company executives received only 20 percent of what they might have made in a good year; but the ten-thousand-member workforce got their paychecks.

Imagine for a moment what decaying and decrepit downtowns in the U.S. might look like if Wal-Mart, Kmart and the other giant discount operations had chosen to build their stores in the center of towns and cities instead of outside of town. Stephen Tindall of The Warehouse Group could have easily copied the American model and built huge stores on cheap land outside of the hundreds of New Zealand and Australian towns and provincial centers where its stores are now located. But Tindall's long-term view was that eventually people would come to hate you for destroying their downtowns. Instead, The Warehouse prefers to build stores smack in the middle of the city. Frequently conducted social audits show that this policy generally finds 80 percent of the other merchants reporting increased sales following the opening of a Warehouse store.

All the highly productive enterprises we studied not only ask WT-GBRFDT but have sufficient patience to also ask "WTG—*long term*—BRFDT?"

6. Disdain for Waste

Any responsible manager, owner or CEO is prepared to discourse at the drop of a hat about the inappropriateness of waste. Yet their remarks have a hollow ring when it becomes obvious their view of waste and indulgence applies to everyone except them.

None of the leaders or cultures we studied fit the definition of cheap or stingy. That being said, each shares disdain for waste. In their own words, each affirms what Herb Sandler says: "It's not *not* spending money that makes you productive and successful, it's the art of *how* you spend money."

For example, while almost all residential mortgage companies continue to slash overhead expenses by focusing on automated underwriting and appraisals, World Savings continues to spend tens of millions annually on its own staff of in-house appraisers. Why? "Because," according to Herb Sandler, "the higher costs associated with our in-house staff are more than made up by the high quality of our loan portfolio, and we avoid the high costs associated with lower quality loans." The objective of an appraisal at World Savings is to increase the likelihood that if a borrower defaults the company will be able to quickly sell the property and recoup its investment. By spending more money than its competitors appraising homes, the company hasn't had a single charge-off for bad loans in the past five years.

All seventy thousand members of the IKEA workforce are thoroughly grounded in the Swedish concept of *"lista,"* a term Ingvar Kamprad loves to write and talk about. The word comes from the stony province of Småland in southern Sweden where, according to Kamprad, the people have a long tradition of making do with what they have.

In IKEA terms, he explains, "lista" might mean lowering a shelf eighteen inches so you can continue to use a hand-operated pallet truck, rather than running out to purchase a new forklift. Or, giving another example, he says, "It might mean making do with a padlock until a permanent lock is repaired."

Unless leaders practice frugality and thrift themselves, they can't infuse this trait into their businesses.

7. Coach Leadership

The role of the manager, owner or CEO as the guardian of heritage, assets and culture has largely been replaced with an ethos of fast leverage and quick results at any cost.

What we found in common among all the cultures of our selected companies was that the CEOs view their role as that of a teacher. These leaders were eager to share values and insights with those around them, rather than behave as Old World command-and-control autocrats.

Bill Zollars frequently compares his job to that of a coach, and every other outstanding leader also acknowledged the vital role of being a mentor/coach. Marion Sandler says her biggest thrill is playing mentor. So serious is Jack Stack about his teaching and coaching role that he's institutionalized the practice in the twenty-two companies that make up SRC; all SRC managers and executives are responsible for having three people trained and prepared to take over their job. (By striving for three, Stack admits, he generally gets two.)

8. Humility

The downplaying of one's own self is a long-forgotten value that's been replaced with enough self-indulgent, self-promoting horn tooting to drown out the noise of those seventy-six trombones. Ask any PR manager how much of his or her time is used to promote the image of the company leaders. The excuse is that everything is show biz; believe me, that's just an excuse.

One of the executives at World Savings we were directed to for accurate numbers is Bill Nunan, the company's chief accounting officer or, as he enjoys saying, "the current holder of the numbers." Although our conversations with Nunan were generally limited to his providing the latest operating numbers and his insistence that he wasn't part of the story, during one conversation he said something that speaks volumes not only about World Savings but all the companies we've included.

"If you can think of one key theme running through our whole company," he said, "it's that the Sandlers recognize that they 'put their pants on one leg at a time,' just like everyone else and ego isn't part of the equation here."

"One of the fears that drives Herb is that he might slip and fall into the trap of smelling his own perfume and forget that his success stems from working hard and staying focused all the time. But, he does work hard everyday and he insists that every single person in the organizations does the same."

"There are no trappings of power here - no fancy offices, exotic cars, expense accounts or names on the doors." Nobody at World, including the Sandlers, puts their ego on anything. There just isn't any time allowed for the indulgence of ego, concluding, "that's one of the key reasons this place works like a charm."

You'd guess that breathing life into a moribund steel company would present many huge challenges, and one Ken Iverson remembers especially well was when he decided that everyone would wear one color hard hat. Iverson's interest in creating an egalitarian culture had been piqued one day when he read a newspaper story from Canada about a factory where they had adopted this practice, and he promptly decided to do the same at Nucor.

Prior to Iverson's decision, everyone in the factory wore a different-colored hard hat depending on the position he held. Workers wore one color, supervisors another and foremen still another. When someone from the home office went to visit a plant they were, Iverson says, "if you can believe this display of ego, given a gold helmet to wear."

Later, in his book, *Plain Talk,* Iverson wrote that keeping his new policy of white hard hats for everyone (except safety personnel) faced more opposition than almost any decision he ever made. "My phone didn't stop ringing," he recounts. "'You can't do that,' they'd say to me, 'My helmet tells everyone who I am and my position.'" Iverson was dismayed to discover just how preoccupied most people are about status and ego.

Straight-talking Pat Lancaster sums up the rightful place for ego when he says, "This place works because of the collaborative efforts of everyone. We have no time or place for self-absorbed egotists."

9. Rejection of Bureaucracy

Anyone who heads a division or a company probably has a prepared statement and press release espousing their commitment to dismantling bureaucratic structures. But bureaucracy sure seems to exist at most companies. (Call your long-distance carrier, health insurance provider, brokerage firm, automobile manufacturer or the company that made your kitchen appliances and ask a frontline customer service representative for the name, address and telephone number of their supervisor, the VP responsible for their operating unit and the CEO. You'll not only be stonewalled by a labyrinth-like bureaucratic structure filled with nameless and faceless managers who want nothing to do with you, but along the way you'll encounter people prepared to become really nasty in defending the anonymity of everyone above them.)

We alternately wondered whether the disdain for bureaucracy shared by the leaders of our group of leading companies was a manifestation of problems they'd encountered with a bureaucratic structure sometime during their career or whether they'd seen ponderous structures slow down good ideas, products and services.

What we learned, though, was that their eagerness to eliminate bureaucracy is a natural, almost instinctive reaction because of the other personality traits they exhibit. Bureaucracies waste money, show disrespect for workers, destroy competitive spirits and don't fit the goal of *simple*.

Pat Lancaster's comment about waste accurately sums up the way these leaders all feel about bureaucracies and the antibureaucratic cultures of their companies. "Anything that doesn't add value is waste, and leadership's responsibility is to eliminate it."

10. Belief in Others

Almost everyone would agree that while belief in the abilities and worth of others is admirable, it doesn't happen in most American workplaces.

When people are truly valued and are given an understanding of the connection between what they do and the ultimate success of the company, they feel involved in determining how to become more productive. They also feel safe and secure from the threat of layoffs, downsizing and nonstop reorganizations.

Bill Zollars at Yellow encourages people to make mistakes, Ingvar Kamprad's IKEA entrusts stores with $25 million in sales to managers in their mid-twenties and Nucor encourages teams of workers to play with equipment worth tens of millions of dollars in hopes of optimizing production. These actions make it obvious to all workers that these leaders share a belief in others.

During my research and writing, I was frequently asked by students, clients, friends and neighbors, "What companies are you writing about and what are some of the things you're finding?" I always searched my memory bank for something certain to elicit a positive response. Early in our research we learned of the sick-pay policy at The Warehouse Group. It's a simple policy. When you're sick, stay home and they'll pay you, whether you're off for a week with the flu, recovering for weeks from a broken leg or battling cancer for months. All the company asks of its workers is that unless they're really sick, they show up for work. It's a tidy little policy that doesn't require legions of manuals and HR administrators.

What was of particular interest to me was the reaction I received from people when I explained that policy. Not one person said, "That makes sense to me." Without exception their reaction was a universal "You couldn't do that in the United States because nobody would ever show up for work and they'd lie and say they were sick all the time. They'd bankrupt the company." Their reactions speak volumes about the fact that most people outside highly productive cultures don't "get" what intrinsically makes these outstanding companies function far ahead of all others: a steadfast belief that when treated fairly, people will do the right thing.

11. Trust

Finally, trust may be the trickiest one of the traits because the word itself elicits a question. Who goes first? Does the manager trust people first and then wait to be trusted? Or should employees and workers trust first while patiently waiting to earn the trust of their supervisors and bosses? And why would such a question even need to be asked? Trust either is or is not. When trust is grudgingly doled out—the rare gold star for good behavior—it's not trust but manipulation; it is condescending, disrespectful and unfair. Your people will find you out sooner rather than later.

The leaders of all the companies we studied begin by trusting people. Their trust is almost always returned and they are seldom disappointed. *Herb trusted me from beginning*

Making the Eleven Traits Your Own

Question: If someone matches the profile we've built, does it automatically mean she's destined to build and lead a productive enterprise?

Answer: No!

Question: If someone doesn't possess the traits described, is he capable of founding and directing a hugely productive company?

Answer: We think . . . probably not.

We'll never fully know why and how the founders and managers of the productive enterprises we studied came to share these eleven personality traits, but each of the traits is by now also embedded into the cultures of the companies they created.

Was Marion Sandler raised by doting parents who led her to believe she could accomplish anything? When confronted with "You're a woman so you'll never be a partner," did she adopt an "I'll show them" spirit of competitiveness? How did Stephen Tindall, who admits to a brief flirtatious admiration of socialism as a youth, come to have such complete disregard for bureaucracy? And what were the circumstances that led Ken Iverson to proclaim a policy of no layoffs? As an engineer, did he run some numbers to arrive at his decision or did he simply believe it was the right thing to do?

It's been said that everyone has to stand for something, that the alternative is to stand for nothing. Whether the values these people share and embody within their companies are a result of genetics, environment or a life's journey that delivered them a few kicks in the butt isn't important. The more important questions are:

- Can these traits be learned, adopted and practiced by others?
- Can someone take the traits that describe the highly productive cultures and embody them within another organization?

The answer to both questions is yes . . . but only by people prepared to begin the journey by fully understanding and becoming determined to make each trait their own.

No leader can build a culture of people paying attention to detail unless they lead the way. A leader can't build a fiercely competitive enterprise while hiding comfortably within the confines of a plush office. If truth is to be a core value, then every manager must have the ability to say it like it is. Ditto for building a company with the principles of simplicity, disdain for waste, a coaching-collegial environment, a humble workplace and trust.

If Shakespeare is right that the word often precedes the action, then people can grow to behave in admirable ways as a result of expressing the virtues they want to achieve. In an ideal world, leaders would already possess the eleven traits; lacking that, the words and the expressed values may help leaders as well as workers to grow into these virtuous behaviors. Here's another interpretation of the old question "Which came first, the chicken or the egg?" Good things happen both ways.

The eleven traits embodied in highly productive leaders and cultures are an admirable list of inspirational words. If these words are used from behind the podium at a success rally they're probably capable of bringing the audience to their feet with a rousing standing ovation. But these traits aren't easy to adopt, master and embody. With the exception of a single trait—competitiveness—the other ten traits defy conventional wisdom and anyone adopting them will find they're swimming upstream against a strong current much of the time. It takes patience and determination for a leader to infuse them into a culture and make these traits the infrastructure of his company. It takes as much determination and patience as building a fit body from a flabby one. Maybe more.

Institutionalizing the Traits of Leadership

When someone says, "That person has integrity," they're generally using the term as a synonym for truth, honesty and frankness. While such contemporary usage is correct, it doesn't take into consideration the origin of the word.

For thousands of years the word "integrity" was used as an engineering term. When a building wasn't safe to occupy or a bridge could no longer support a load, both were said to have lost their structural integrity. Integrity actually means wholeness and completeness. The leaders of truly productive companies have absolute integrity and remain true to what they believe—all the time, not just when convenience allows.

The words and phrases that describe leaders and the cultures they've built are appropriate and apt all the time. Not only on good Mondays and at ball games, not only when the stock prices are up and profits are streaming in, not only when it's a good hair day or when a golf score is exactly where it should be. People who can be counted on to think and react the same way all the time can be described as having integrity. Honesty is being honest when no one's looking. There are a few rare people who can be the same when talking to one person across a desk as when being interviewed on TV with three million viewers watching.

There's probably no more insidious phrase than "Do as I say, not as I do." A young child hearing it from a parent is certain to become confused and frustrated. A teenager will express resentment and anger. The statement doesn't have to be spoken out loud; we all know how easy it is to spot the hypocrite who expects us to behave one way while he or she behaves another, and we recognize the attitude as patronizing, arrogant and dismissive.

Business leaders worth following are people who lead by demonstrating their own ethical behavior. They are the leaders who consistently prove the proposition that *Less Is More*, setting the model and the tone for the culture of their organizations.

Building a Culture

The winning companies and people profiled in these pages lead the ranks of the world's most productive entrepreneurs; by now you've come to realize that their outstanding success isn't due to a series of slick manipulative tricks or sly tactics.

Each of these leaders used essentially the same steps in creating a highly successful organization. As we've seen, each in his or her own way—

- Began with a BIG objective
- Got everyone onboard and then proceeded to streamline everything by ruthlessly fighting to keep the business proposition simple
- Communicated truthfully with everyone
- Cleaned out the management ranks of those unable, unprepared or unwilling to go where the enterprise was headed
- Demonstrated the way they value people by policies of no layoffs
- Institutionalized *What's the good business reason for doing this?*
- Measured and shared the real Drivers with everyone
- Turned every business process into a best-practices system designed to eliminate waste
- Committed to a program of continual improvement
- Paid people for productivity in ways that drive the culture, and
- Employed the right technology to gain a productive edge.

A Final Word and Cause for Hope: You Can Make It Happen.

I'm hopeful that readers will finish my books having had both conventional wisdom and their own thinking challenged, having gained new levels of understanding and freshly sharpened skills. The last thing I'd want is for a reader to finish this book and walk away believing or saying, "They sound like great companies, which is great for them but what in the hell am I supposed to do? I'm stuck in midmanagement and my fossil-filled company is never going to get it or let me do it."

If that's an accurate description of what's going on in your company, there are still several options available to you:

- You can begin by adopting the principles described in this chapter and implementing them quietly in the group or department you're responsible for;
- You can initiate a job search and join another company with a strong, uplifting, productive culture like those described here;
- You can strike out on your own (as did the founders of World Savings, IKEA and The Warehouse) with firm resolve to create a highly ethical and productive company; or
- You can wait for the opportunity to help transform your present company, remembering that when companies fall on hard times (like Yellow, Lantech, SRC, Ryanair, Nucor), they're open and receptive to change.

As you're deciding what to do with the new information you've learned, there's nothing to stop you from modeling yourself after the principles and traits of this most remarkable group of leaders and enterprises.

EPILOGUE

One of the few indulgences in my modest life is having a personal trainer. I probably wouldn't work out at all if I didn't have someone constantly barking at me and prodding me on. Noah, my trainer, is a thirty-year-old family man armed with a master's degree and great conversational skills. Mostly, though, we just taunt each other.

Every so often, I would tell him what I was writing about. And the further into the book I got, the more interested Noah would become. One day he said, "I think I'm going to like this book more than your last one."

I asked why.

"All the companies sound like great places to work," he said. "Almost like they're giant communes."

I was bench-pressing at that moment, and I nearly dropped the weights on my chest. "What the hell do you mean by communes?" I thundered, racking the weights. "These are some of the most profitable companies in the world. That's how they got in the book. What's this commune garbage?"

As a buttoned-down entrepreneur who has often railed against any -ism other than capitalism, I see a commune as a place where stoner guys with scruffy sandals hang out with earth-mother types, listening to flutes and prancing through meadows.

"Think about it," Noah said. "First you wrote about the importance of the culture of these companies. What's the culture of most American companies? Greed.

"The other chapters are about trust and respect, listening to and involving the workers, paying teams instead of individuals, making everything a system, eliminating waste, creating egalitarian environments," he said. "They sound like wonderful communes to me."

I could only imagine the way the hard-driving leaders of these enterprises would react to Noah's analogy. Yet the comparison fascinated me. And shortly afterward, some college-age readers reinforced it.

"These are really cool companies. How did you find them?" was a nearly unanimous response.

Many people experience the same distaste for corporations that I feel for communes. The news is full of reports of shredding at Enron, fraud at WorldCom, Kmart ripping apart at the seams and CEOs at money-losing companies who pay themselves multimillion-dollar bonuses. To some, then, the companies described in this book may sound idyllic.

But these businesses are not communes. They're pragmatic, profitable companies headed by humble people whose egalitarian values support their business goals. The leaders of the great companies know that a really good deal is one in which everyone wins.

In summary, here are the rules that buck conventional wisdom, as practiced by the iconoclasts who lead some of the world's most productive enterprises.

Twelve Rules for Doing More with Less

- Start with a simple proposition. Don't let anyone—even you—muck it up by making it too complicated. If it's already complicated, simplify it.
- Spend your time building a culture, not a business model—one based on truth, honesty and respect. Be authentic and live the values.
- Make certain that every manager and executive believes and practices everything on this list or get rid of him or her imme-

diately. He isn't necessarily a bad person, but he is the wrong person.

- Ask WTGBRFDT—"What's the good business reason for doing this?"—of every decision you're called on to make. Don't delude yourself.
- Get rid of special perks for executives. They earn enough to pay for their own indulgences. Class distinctions make people jealous.
- Enter into a covenant that layoffs and head-count reduction won't be used as a tool to cover up management's bad decisions, poor judgment calls and mistakes.
- Teach everyone business and have everyone understand the direct relationship between their work and the financial well-being of the enterprise. If a direct connection can't be made, keep the worker but eliminate the position.
- Put everyone on a team and pay the teams for what they create, produce, sell or service. Let peer pressure drive out the dead-beats.
- Turn every function into a system and map it out. Then constantly ask the people who do the work how to eliminate waste and make the system better.
- Implement your new processes quickly and perform them over and over again, working each time to eliminate waste.
- Be competitive and keep score. It keeps things fun.
- Embrace technology, but don't count on it for a competitive advantage. Everyone else can have the same technology.

An Invitation

If you ever attend one of my speeches or lectures, please take the time to introduce yourself and spend a few minutes with me. I'm genuinely thrilled to meet my readers, to learn what you're thinking and hear what you have to say.

Finally, you're invited to visit Jennings-solutions.com, where you'll find an entire section devoted to the subject of *Less Is More* and the opportunity to take part in one of our weekly live interactive sessions on the subject.

Best wishes.

ACKNOWLEDGMENTS

For this book I was fortunate in being able to assemble and work with a dream team of people who share my guiding principle that no one is more important than the reader.

My gratitude and sincere thanks are offered in *chronological* order to all the team members who "built" this book. If a book jacket were large enough, each would be receiving coauthor credit.

Laurence Haughton, my coauthor on the last book, who has been a valuable colleague for almost two decades.

Alan Nevins of Artist Management Group, whose guidance and direction have been invaluable.

When Adrian Zackheim agreed to publish my first book at his former publishing company, I promised him that taking a chance on me wouldn't be forgotten. I'm proud to work for him and have his belief and support. The insights and help offered by Bill Brazell, senior editor at Portfolio, were always on target. Many thanks also to copy editor Noirin Lucas and production editor Bruce Giffords for their invaluable advice and guidance.

Greg Powell was the lead researcher on the book and he's one of the most talented men I've ever had the opportunity to work with. The very organization of the book is owed to him. The guy's got mojo.

I'd also like to thank Greg's research team: Marisa Rolland, a Stanford graduate with degrees in international relations and French literature, and Yinh Hinh, a Berkeley graduate in interdisciplinary studies.

For ten years Bruce Ritter of San Rafael, California, has served as my family's investment counselor and during that time he's also become a trusted adviser on all aspects of my career. He contributed his keen analytical abilities to every aspect of the book.

I'd also like to thank William L. Simon, whose thinking, tinkering, organizational skills and incredible talent with words opened my mind to new collaborations; surely we'll work on future projects together.

Among the world's most productive companies, I'd like to thank the following for their extraordinary candor and generosity: Jack Stack, the CEO of SRC Holdings; Becky lane, Jack Stack's executive assistant; Dianna Devore, CEO of Megavolt (an SRC Holdings company); Dan DiMicco, CEO of Nucor; Pat Lancaster, chairman of Lantech; Rita Clark, Pat Lancaster's executive assistant; Jean Cunningham, CFO of Lantech; James Lancaster, president of Lantech; Herb and Marion Sandler, co-CEOs of World Savings; Linda Barrett, executive assistant to Herb and Marion Sandler; Bill Nunan, CAO of World Savings; Michael O'Leary, CEO of Ryanair; Stephen Tindall, chairman of The Warehouse Group; Greg Muir, CEO of The Warehouse Group; Kent Nordin, country manager for IKEA Australia; Lars-Goran Petersson, IKEA purchasing coordination; Thomas Bergmark, IKEA environmental and social manager; Lars Engman, design manager for IKEA; Clive Cashman, IKEA public relations; Bill Zollars, CEO of Yellow Corp.; Greg Reid, chief marketing officer and senior vice president of Yellow; Cheryl Billington, vice president of systems at Yellow; Suzanne Dawson, Yellow public relations; and Jim Ritchie, CEO of Meridian IQ (a Yellow Corporation company).

Then there were the other people who helped us, including Anand Sharma, CEO and president of TBM Consulting; James Womack, president and founder of the Lean Enterprise Institute; Chet Marchwinski, director of communications for the Lean Enterprise Institute; Ed Constantine, chairman of Simpler Consulting; Bruce Thompson, cofounder and vice president of consulting services for

Simpler Consulting; Bob Rosinski, senior partner at Anitech; Orest Fiume, vice president of finance at Wiremold; Lars Nyberg, CEO of NCR; Jeff Dafler, public relations with NCR; the Graduate School of Business and the Jackson Library at Stanford University; Harvard Business School Press; Rob Tai; Dr. Linda Trevino, professor of ethics and chairwoman of the Department of Management and Organization at Smeal College, Pennsylvania State University; Daniel W. Rasmus, vice president of Giga Information Group; Victor Infante, journalist; Jack Nilles, consultant with JALA International; Alison Bartlett; Dr. Eliyahu Goldratt, writer; David Cay Johnston, New York Times journalist; Dr. Salvador Aceves, San Francisco State University Business School professor; Tom Faulkner, community relations with NUMMI; Alfie Kohn, author of Punished by Rewards; Dr. James Campbell Quick, University of Texas at Arlington professor of organizational behavior and director of the doctoral program in business administration; Brent Hendrix, production manager for Allison Transmission (a GM division); Dr. Jeffrey Pfeffer, Thomas D. Dee II Professor of Organizational Behavior at the Stanford University Graduate School of Business; Alan Cramb, codirector of the Center for Iron and Steelmaking Research at Carnegie Mellon University; William Mercer Consulting; Bain & Company; McKinsey & Company; Janet Dang; Gary Moore, a senior vice president at Cisco; and Lieutenant General Don Johnson USAF (retired).

Several astute businesspeople generously offered to review chapters: Jane Hennessy, senior vice president of Wells Fargo Bank; Chuck Adams, CFO of Innergy Corporation; and Dave Trabert, vice president of KAKE Television.

Thanks to Pat Martin, our tireless transcription typist; Noah Wickliffe of Body Image in Mill Valley, California; and George Staubli.

There are four other people whose guidance it gives me great pleasure to acknowledge. Vince Thompson, VP of AOL Time Warner;

Pat Shaughnessy, CEO of AVI Communications in Dallas, Texas; Marc and Jon Reede of Nationwide Speakers, the agents who book my speeches.

I also offer my heartfelt thanks to my family. Researching and writing a book is a family affair because the researcher/author needs support and understanding during an extraordinarily stressful time. For many months "the book *rules*" was the family motto. As always, my family members were there for me. Now, it's their turn to have my full attention.

Finally, thanks to you, the reader, for buying this volume. Without you there's no need for researchers, authors and books.

INDEX